Questions you ask about SEX

LYNETTE EVANS
&
HELEN JACKSON

answer

Questions you ask about SEX

VIKING O'NEIL

Viking O'Neil
Penguin Books Australia Ltd
487 Maroondah Highway, P.O. Box 257
Ringwood, Victoria 3134, Australia
Penguin Books Ltd
Harmondsworth, Middlesex, England
Viking Penguin Inc.
40 West 23rd Street, New York, N.Y. 10010, U.S.A.
Penguin Books Canada Limited
2801 John Street, Markham, Ontario, Canada L3R 1B4
Penguin Books (N.Z.) Ltd
182–190 Wairau Road, Auckland 10, New Zealand

10 9 8 7 6 5 4 3 2 1

Produced by Viking O'Neil
56 Claremont Street, South Yarra, Victoria 3141, Australia
A division of Penguin Books Australia Ltd

Design by Sandra Nobes
Cover design by David Constable
Cover photographs by Lynette Zeeng, Simon Bullard
Typeset in Cheltenham by Bookset Pty Ltd, Victoria
Printed by Australian Print Group, Maryborough, Victoria

National Library of Australia
Cataloguing-in-Publication data

Evans, Lynette.
    Lynette Evans and Helen Jackson answer questions you ask
    about sex.

    Bibliography.
    ISBN 0 670 90129 6.

    1. Sex instruction. 2. Sex counselling. I. Jackson, Helen (Helen
    Jane). II. Title. III. Title: Questions you ask about sex.

306.7

Contents

Introduction

For five years, on 3AW Melbourne, we ran a weekly talkback program about sex. During that time we discussed a diverse range of fascinating topics. Some were fun, some were sad. Others, like 'How do I make love to my wife with her two cats watching us? One sits on top of the wardrobe and the other on the bed and it puts me off!', were sometimes difficult to take seriously!

However, what surprised us most was that listeners repeatedly asked for information about such basic sexual issues as orgasm, masturbation and contraception. Another great cause for anxiety among many male listeners was whether or not their penises were normal!

We found that for years people had carried around with them fears and doubts about sex which they'd never discussed with anyone — either from embarrassment or from uncertainty about where to go for help. A talkback program like ours was ideal for them because they could talk one-to-one about their problems, and still remain anonymous.

We came to the conclusion that requests from many of our listeners for basic sexual information were no reflection on them, but rather a reflection on the way such information is usually presented. In some cases it is not presented at all, because it *is* so basic.

We perceived the need for a frank, down-to-earth book to fill this gap, which is why we have written *Questions you ask about Sex*. As the title suggests, it is based on what our listeners most often wanted to know and includes many questions asked on air.

On our program we aimed to:

- identify the problem
- outline what we believed the person could do about it (this sometimes included suggesting the caller see a qualified therapist or doctor)
- back up our information with suggested reading matter.

We have followed a similar policy in this book and have included lists of recommended reading and support organisations.

Where a medical problem is involved we have recommended that you see a doctor. Fortunately, doctors who mutter into their stethoscopes about the weather or cheerfully tell you 'You shouldn't worry about that sort of thing at your age', when asked sexual questions, are ever so slowly disappearing from the scene. However, our program received constant reminders of the lack of training general practitioners had had in this area in the past. The callers were unhappy either about the medical advice or the treatment they received. If you are not satisfied, always get a second or even a third opinion and never be afraid to question your doctor until you understand your condition and the treatment.

For certain other problems we have recommended you consult a psychologist. If you decide to do so, make sure the person you see has a post-graduate degree in clinical psychology or at least belongs to the clinical division of the Australian Psychological Society. Check that he or she is qualified before you make an appointment. We make no apology for this advice, because many people practise without these qualifications.

Chapter One

Protecting Yourself

Comedian Woody Allen has a wonderful line about what he calls oral contraception:

'I asked a girl to go to bed with me and she said "No".'

No sex may be the safest form of contraception — oral or otherwise — but it is not much fun, and in Woody's case did nothing for the future of the relationship. However, Woody's anecdote is an excellent example of good, clear communication, which is very important when you set out to find the protection that is just right for you and your partner.

It is very important that a book about sex starts with the subject of protection because it is the very first thing that you should work out in a new relationship. Even though you may be feeling overwhelmingly attracted to each other and can hardly wait to make love, you must ask yourselves a decidedly unromantic question:

'Have we got adequate contraception?'

Ideally, you must sort out this (and protection against sexually transmitted diseases, as we will discuss later) with a new sexual partner *before* you get to the heavy breathing stage. Yet many couples, particularly young people, shy away from such issues as if they have been blessed with some inbuilt, God-given immunity to pregnancy.

The unwanted pregnancy rate for teenagers in Australia is extremely high. This is certainly not due to lack of available information. Schools and parents are more aware than ever before of the importance of contraception for young adults, and are more open about discussing them. Health clinics give out free advice on the subject, and hospitals' and doctors' waiting rooms display free, easy-to-read leaflets.

It is easy to dismiss people who 'risk it' (and they are not all teenagers) as irresponsible daredevils with an 'I'll be all right' attitude. But this is too simplistic — they are more likely to be normal, intelligent, caring people. The next morning, these same people probably worry themselves sick about the consequences of the night before.

So why is there such a reluctance in our society to discuss protection? It seems that the *real* problem is that people are so uneasy talking about sex to a partner that they would prefer to risk pregnancy or even a serious or possibly fatal sexually transmitted disease (STD) than discuss precautions. Evidence of this behaviour has shown up in recent research about the non-use of condoms in relation to acquired immune deficiency syndrome (AIDS) and other STDs. People do not want to talk about it.

We believe the answer to the problem lies in greater acceptance of ourselves as sexual beings. We must accept that we have sexual needs in the same way that we accept we have to be fed and clothed and housed for our well-being. Information alone is not sufficient. We have got to feel okay about the sexual part of ourselves.

Part of accepting your sexual self is being able to discuss your needs with your partner. This can be very difficult to do with a new partner, but it is essential to discuss contraception at the start of a sexual relationship. The at-the-time methods of contraception, which we discuss below, require very good communication skills, but, even though the long-term methods do not demand as much discussion at the time of sex, it's essential that you and your partner talk about such an important aspect of your relationship as contraception.

In our section on the condom as an at-the-time method, we show you how you can initiate and build on a conversation about contraception. You will find that just by pushing yourself to say something, when you would normally have remained silent about sex, gives you enormous confidence to continue to improve yourself in this area. Even if you think your communication skills are bad and you know that you are not as comfortable with your sexuality as you would like to be, to have even begun a conversation is a huge leap forward. After this it is simply a matter of continuing to push the new you into saying things, where the old one would have remained silent. A good idea is to *look* for opportunities to ask questions and share information about sex with your partner. Be fair and understanding, but very honest, when you tell him or her how you feel about anything he or she does. You could not have a better basis for a relationship than one where, with trust and respect, each partner lets the other know what he or she wants and how he or she feels. If you can do it with sexual information, it will be easy to do it in all other areas of the relationship and that will give you a very satisfying time together. Believe us!

Now we will discuss contraception and protection in more detail.

Broadly, contraception falls into two categories: methods you can use at the time of intercourse, such as condoms, diaphragms and spermicides; and long-term methods, such as fertility awareness, the Pill, intra-uterine devices and sterilisation.

Our discussion of at-the-time methods begins with condoms because when you have sex with a new partner you should always use a condom. After sophisticated contraceptives, such as the Pill, became available about a quarter of a century ago, condoms were pushed into the background. However, with the spread of STDs, and the advent of AIDS in particular, it was rapidly realised that the humble condom was not only a reliable form of contraception, but also one of the most effective methods of protection against STDs.

Many of the STDs prevalent today can be hard to treat and can have serious effects on your health and relationships. A number can cause painful intercourse, infertility and abnormalities and death in the newborn; a few are potentially fatal. Diseases that can be sexually transmitted include chlamydia, genital herpes, trichomoniasis, genital warts, thrush, gonorrhoea, syphilis and AIDS. For information about STDs refer to the Recommended Reading list and STD clinics given under Support Organisations at the end of the book.

Obviously, everybody needs to know about STDs today, since they can have such a major effect on health, sexual relationships and family life. (Even if you are in a long-term relationship your situation may change in the future or you may need to advise a family member or friend.) But you also need to know that, if you are able to recognise exactly when you may be at risk — for example, at the start of a new relationship — and if you use a condom to protect yourself, you can enjoy safe and happy sex.

AT-THE-TIME CONTRACEPTIVE METHODS

CONDOMS

Used correctly (see below), condoms can be a most effective form of contraception. They can also be combined with other methods of contraception, such as spermicides and fertility awareness. As well as offering protection against STDs, condoms are often the most satisfactory form of contraception when long-term methods do not answer your need for immediate contraception or are inappropriate at the start of a new relationship.

But how to tell a new partner you want to use a condom? The honest answer to this is with difficulty and a measure of embarrassment. Still, that is a small price to pay for the peace of mind you will have once you have been brave enough to raise the matter.

Although you will be anxious, if you can just start the conversation it should not be hard to continue. In fact it should get easier from then on. You could say something like:

'I feel very sexually attracted to you and I want to have sex, but I would like us to use a condom. How do you feel about that?'

As brief as it seems, given most circumstances, this statement should be enough to open up the subject and you will be able to suggest to your new partner why you want to use this method of contraception and that you want to protect yourself from STDs. Despite the difficulty and embarrassment, it is absolutely worth the effort of adding something like this to your conversation with your new partner:

'Even though we are attracted to each other, we do not know each other very well yet, so for both our sakes I would like us to use a condom.'

If your new partner is understanding and considerate, you will not have much trouble working out what you both want to do.

Of course, it will be a different story if your partner reacts in an unreasonable way. You will need to be more prepared for this. The first thing to remember is not to get flustered by a negative or overly surprised reaction. Keep calm and say something like:

'I can understand you reacting this way, and perhaps a condom is not your favourite form of contraception, but at the moment it is the one I would like to use.'

If you still cannot reach an agreement, be reassuring about your feelings for your partner, but firm about your wish to use a condom by saying something like:

'I would like to work this out, but I am not prepared to go along with something I am uneasy about. I know I will only regret it later. Let's talk about it in a couple of days.'

Then just do something together that you both enjoy and which does not involve you getting into a situation where you want sex again. By this time, though, sex will probably be the furthest thing from your mind. Try not to let the conversation about contraception end your time together.

Make sure you discuss contraception together again before you get into another sexual situation. If you are both well-intentioned, you should find a suitable solution. But never go along with something that makes you feel unhappy.

To be effective, condoms must be properly applied.

Putting on a condom can become part of a couple's foreplay, with the woman helping the man to roll it down over his penis.

The saying 'practice makes perfect' couldn't be more apt for condom use. Before you get into a sexual encounter it would be worth the few extra dollars and the time to practise putting on a condom. The following steps should ensure effective use:

- check the date on the packet of condoms to ensure that they are not out of date
- carefully undo the wrapping around a condom without tearing or nicking the contents in any way
- make sure you pinch the teat at the top of the condom and that you have the rolled-up edge facing outwards
- push out the air in the teat, as this is where the sperm

6

goes and the condom could burst if air remains when ejaculation occurs

- roll the condom down over the fully erect penis — it is important to make sure the penis *is* fully erect
- never start intercourse until the condom is on, as small amounts of seminal fluid can leak out of the penis *before* ejaculation — for this reason the man's penis should be nowhere near his partner's vagina during the arousal stage
- after ejaculation hold the base of the condom so that it doesn't unroll, withdraw the penis from the vagina while it is still *erect* — don't wait until it has started to shrink again, because sperm can leak out of the condom into the woman's vagina
- dispose of the condom in an appropriate way and make sure you never use the same condom again.

Some men object to the feel of condoms; some women also complain that they cut down sensitivity. If this is the case (and you are using the condom purely as a contraceptive), you can work out a compromise where it is only used during the woman's fertile period. The time of fertility varies in each woman, but generally it lasts up to ten days. So there could be about eighteen days of her cycle when you don't need to use a condom. In order to do this, you must both learn to identify her fertile times, with the help of a natural family planning clinic, the Family Planning Association clinics, sexual guidance clinics at major hospitals or your doctor. Obviously, co-operation and good communication are very important for this to work, but the benefits make it a most worthwhile thing to master.

As we have said, spermicides can also be used with condoms if a couple feel they want added protection, particularly around a fertile time. They come in either foam or suppository form and are readily available at chemist shops.

The above general information on condoms also applies to male homosexual couples. They can also use spermicides as a lubricant or, if they prefer, they can get an appropriate water-soluble lubricant, such as KY Jelly, from a chemist. (Oil-based lubricants such as Vaseline can weaken the latex in the condom.)

If, after reading all this, you are still uncertain about either the correct use of a condom or whether or not to use one, go to someone who can explain it to you personally. You will find trained people at any Family Planning Association clinic. Your doctor may help, or even a friendly chemist could explain the finer points of condom need and use. It is essential to know about these things if you are going to be fully protected against pregnancy and STDs.

DIAPHRAGM AND CERVICAL CAP

Both are barrier methods used by the woman, and both require an appointment with a doctor, because they need to be correctly fitted. Whichever you have chosen to use is then inserted before intercourse, and must be left in for a time afterwards.

Spermicides are used with both the diaphragm and the cap to increase their efficiency. If the couple makes love more than once during, say, an evening the spermicide must be reapplied.

SPERMICIDES

These can be used on their own as a contraceptive, although it is probably not advisable to do so; they are at their most effective when used with other barrier methods such as the condom, cervical cap or diaphragm. They can be bought over the counter in a chemist shop and are easy to apply.

LONG-TERM METHODS

FERTILITY AWARENESS (OR NATURAL FAMILY PLANNING)

The essential factors for this method to work are that the woman is very motivated and that she has a co-operative partner. If these two requirements are met, it can be an extremely effective form of contraception.

Ideally, the couple should go along to a clinic that specialises in natural family planning, which is also called the rhythm method, or the Billings method of identifying the woman's fertile period. If you can't go as a couple, it is all right for the woman to go alone. But you must both be happy with this method.

The clinic will instruct you, and also monitor the woman's progress. When the woman is in her fertile period she and her partner can use one of the barrier methods of contraception, but when she is not, there is no need to use any protection.

HORMONAL

These include the combined contraceptive Pill, the progestogen-only Pill, the morning-after Pill and progestogen injections (including Depo-provera). These can only be obtained on prescription from a doctor. It is, therefore, necessary for you to have a consultation if you think one of these may be right for you. It is just as necessary to make sure that you and your partner are fully aware of the potential benefits and long-term risks associated with each of them. Ask your doctor all the questions you can possibly think of before deciding to go ahead. Make a list of questions if you're afraid you may forget some of them once you get inside the doctor's surgery.

Most doctors tend to have a bias towards a particular type of contraception, so in order to get a wider range of opinions you may have to visit a couple of doctors before making your decision.

This could certainly be a nuisance, but if you are willing to persevere you will be better off in the long run. At the very least it will prevent your being persuaded by only one doctor's bias. After all it is *your* body so it's surely worth a bit of effort to find out about the most suitable form of hormonal contraceptive, one that is going to put you at least risk and give you maximum benefit.

Another point to remember is that there is no such thing as the perfect contraceptive. There will be pros and cons to be weighed up by you and your partner — even about the method you finally decide upon.

The morning-after Pill is not a regular form of contraception. It is available for use in emergencies, when you think you have risked pregnancy, and is more a form of abortion. It has to be used within a short time after intercourse.

IUD

The IUD or intra-uterine device must be fitted by a doctor. There have been some serious health problems associated with IUD use, so it is very important to make sure you are fully aware of the risks it poses.

STERILISATION

Male or female sterilisation requires an operation. It is probably an easier operation for men to have, and in some cases it can be reversed in the male. Obviously, you and your partner need to seriously weigh up the consequences. You must talk to your doctor about the possibility of reversal *before* you have the operation. However, don't be put off by the negative opinions which seem to abound on this subject. You will find a lot of people willing to give unfounded opinions on sterilisation. Get the facts yourself, then make your *own* decision.

Question

I don't have much feeling when I use a condom. Can you suggest how I can get more satisfaction?

Answer

A man gets satisfaction and reaches orgasm during intercourse because of friction on his penis. This friction, and the sensual feeling it produces, is obviously reduced when he wears a condom. Most people have discovered that the more time they spend on arousal, the faster and often more intense the orgasm. You can apply this information to your advantage when you use a condom. If your partner spends plenty of time arousing you, perhaps helping you to reach the point of orgasm a number of times, you should find the condom less inhibiting in terms of enjoyment and arousal. The stimulation during intercourse should be very intense, even with the condom on.

To get the maximum sensuality out of sex this way it will be necessary for you to encourage your partner to spend as much time as you need during foreplay to arouse you. Your partner will have to be understanding and patient but the benefits will be enormous.

It is probably true to say that, with or without a condom, a man will find it harder to reach an orgasm if he is not fully aroused. There is a big difference between having an erection and being fully aroused, one of the main differences being the man's heightened pleasure; so learning to use condoms as a contraceptive in this way could help couples to have more pleasurable sex — sex that does not place the major emphasis on intercourse, with all the limits that bestows on a couple; sex that puts plenty of emphasis on *both* partners arousing each other. If you run into trouble finding ways to arouse each other, get hold of some books or videos that give you some new, erotic and sensual ideas to try (see also Recommended Reading).

Question

Condoms make me come after only about four minutes of intercourse. That is too quick for my girlfriend to get aroused and have her orgasm.

She doesn't like taking any sort of contraception because of previous trouble with the Pill, so we've resorted to condoms — which really are the easiest and most convenient thing for us.

They're perfect except for this problem. It also takes some of the fun of sex away for both of us to have things over and done with in four minutes. Any advice?

Answer

All you need to do is shift your 'fun' time to just before putting on your condom and having intercourse. In other words, get your girlfriend aroused and to the point of orgasm *before* you enter her. Most women don't have orgasm with intercourse; they get aroused and climax because of stimulation to the clitoris. Four minutes is quite a long time for intercourse to last. Obviously it is not long enough for your girlfriend, so discuss together and explore other ways of turning her on, and spend as much time on this before intercourse as is necessary. If you are happy with the condom, it would be a shame not to persevere for a little while. Who knows, it could have all kinds of sensual, fun side-effects.

Question

I want to buy some condoms, but I can only get as far as the display in the chemist shop, and then I chicken out. I don't think I will need them for a while, but I would like to be prepared, just in case. I am only 16 and still at school. Some friends are having sex with girls without any protection — just hoping the girls are on the Pill. I reckon that's stupid, don't you?

Answer

Congratulations on your sensible attitude! Like you, we'd trade a little embarrassment for an unwanted pregnancy any day.

The first time you pick up the condoms and hand them to the chemist with your money will be the worst, if that is any consolation. You will feel conspicuous, because just buying them implies you are having sex. And, at this stage, sex is not something you are totally relaxed about.

If you can carry through your responsible approach into future relationships, you will be well set up for a satisfying time sexually.

Perhaps discussing your problem with your dad or just another adult you trust would help. Failing that, will yourself to coolly pick up the condoms at the chemist shop. Once you've done it, you'll find it wasn't so terrible! Some supermarkets also carry them now. You might find it easier to hide them under the rest of the groceries. Whichever way you get condoms, make sure you *do* get them so that you can stick to your guns about unprotected sex.

Question

Do you need to have had children to use the IUD successfully? I'm thinking of using it because the Pill strips me of libido — which rather defeats its purpose.

Answer

A trip to your local family planning clinic is probably your best bet. Most doctors will recommend that you have had a pregnancy before using the IUD.

CONTRACEPTION IN SUMMARY

- Get all the information you feel you need.
- Discuss this information with your partner, even if he or she is new.
- Both agree on what you will use, and then try it.
- If one or the other is not happy with the outcome, then change it and try again.

- Make sure you are always prepared to talk about your feelings with your partner. Don't keep them to yourself, no matter how embarrassing it may be.
- When using a condom make sure you spend sufficient time arousing each other.

WHEN CONTRACEPTION FAILS . . .

If your period is overdue and you suspect you may be pregnant, go to your local doctor or clinic immediately. These days it's possible to determine pregnancy within days of a missed period.

If you *are* pregnant you are faced with one of life's most difficult moral dilemmas:

- whether to give birth to an unplanned (and possibly unwanted) baby
- or whether to have an abortion.

Unfortunately, neither alternative is ideal, and no one makes such a decision lightly. It's a case of deciding what's best in the circumstances.

Your decision will be based on your relationship with your partner, your feelings about being parents, your financial position and religious beliefs. Whatever you decide, you'll need to talk it over thoroughly with your partner and/or a reliable friend or relative.

Despite the apparent negativity of having an abortion, it may, nevertheless, be the most positive solution, especially if the pregnancy was not planned. It may be the best solution in the long term, despite the short-term costs.

These short-term costs are the uncertainty, fear and

discomfort about what is involved: uncertainty that it is the *right* thing to do; fear of what others will think or say; and discomfort about the whole procedure of abortion. And, finally, you'll have grave doubts about terminating a new human life.

Nobody would say any of these issues is trivial, particularly the last one. But these short-term considerations have to be weighed against the long-term benefits, the most important of which is NOT bringing an unwanted person into the world. If you do have an unplanned baby, the cost in the long term will be enormous. You will be faced with the awesome responsibility for the welfare and happiness of another human being who will be dependent on you for at least 16 years.

If your pregnancy is unplanned it is essential for you and your partner to think through these issues, whether you have known each other for one night or been married for ten years.

You must work out whether you have the mental, emotional and physical resources to cope with looking after a baby (who will become a child, a teenager, then a young adult). If, for ANY reason, you don't feel equal to taking on this enormous responsibility, it could be argued that it is nothing less than irresponsible for you to proceed with the pregnancy.

This advice may appear cold, but we make no apologies, because it is vital a couple be totally practical about this decision. Too often it is based on sentimental reasons and short-sightedness, rather than on hard, cold reality. Remember, you are doing no one a favour — least of all the baby — to bring an unwanted child into the world.

If you and your partner simply cannot make the decision to terminate the pregnancy — or *not* to terminate it — then get some help. Talk to someone who can set out your options, someone who can be understanding about your feelings, and yet outline your choices, without trying to push you one way or the other. If either of you is at all ambivalent or uncertain about going ahead with the pregnancy, then you are probably better off seeking an abortion.

If one of you wants the baby but the other does not, you have to seriously consider the effects this situation will have on you, the baby and your relationship in the long term. Whatever you do, don't dig in your heels just to make your point, or avoid mentioning the pregnancy until it is too late.

Of course, sometimes the most unpromising situations can work out happily in the end, and many couples have managed to make a go of their relationships, despite an unplanned pregnancy. But in these cases, the two people concerned must be highly motivated to overcome the inevitable obstacles.

ABORTION

Not everyone realises that abortion is legal in Australia, because it is not openly discussed. The procedure varies slightly from state to state, but the first crucial step is to take action early, because the termination must be performed within a specified number of weeks after conception.

Many people have doubts about the safety of abortions because of the days when they were illegal, and poorly qualified people carried out 'back street abortions' under less than ideal conditions. However, today they are performed in modern hospitals and clinics by qualified medical staff, and are considered one of the most straightforward and safe operations.

Probably the easiest and most convenient way to get an abortion is to go to a Family Planning Association clinic, because they usually have counsellors, doctors and a surgery under the one roof.

Make sure it is a family planning clinic that offers abortion, because some clinics that also have the words 'family planning' in their title do *not* provide this operation (and routinely advise against it on religious grounds). So it is best to make sure before you go to the clinic by telephoning and simply asking if they terminate pregnancies (see also Support Organisations). If you have no luck with your family planning clinic, go to your doctor, who will refer you to an appropriate clinic.

Make your first visit to the abortion clinic purely an enquiry visit. Find out *all* you need to know. If you are uncertain about the procedures to be used, ask about them (How is it done?, How safe is it?, What are the associated risks?, etc.). Cover every question, then go away and talk it over with your partner or someone close to you. If possible, speak to a friend who has had an abortion.

If you still feel uncertain, make an appointment with someone who can explain your options in regard to adoption or parenthood. You can do this alone or as a couple. Only after doing all this homework should you finally make your decision to terminate your pregnancy.

You may feel sad and even depressed after an abortion. As we have said, no one makes this decision lightly. Remind yourself that you will feel sad and depressed about what could have been, but that under the circumstances it was really the best decision at the time for everyone — including the foetus.

We have not debated moral or philosophical issues about abortion here because we are more concerned with the practical ones. Abortion is one of the harder facts of life. It is a good argument for contraception and its proper use.

Listeners Share Experiences

I just can't bring myself to talk about contraception with my boyfriend. I feel really silly about it. I know that I am skating on thin ice. I can't go to our doctor for the Pill without my parents finding out. I know we should use condoms.

My girlfriend does want to have sex, but doesn't want to go on the Pill. She doesn't like me using a condom.

This whole situation creates terrible tension between us, so that neither of us has satisfactory sex. We have been going out for six months and both enjoy sex, but the conflict afterwards makes me wonder if it was worth it.

Thirty years ago I went through an unwanted pregnancy. It was an appalling situation because of the ignorance about sexuality in those days. I had to have my baby adopted. Given the choice, I would have had an abortion.

Now I find that my own unmarried daughter is pregnant. I am trying to help her make the right decision for her, but it is extremely difficult not to show my bias and push her towards abortion.

The government legislated during the Second World War to make condom manufacturers put a pin-hole in every one-hundredth condom, and that is why condoms are not safe. I know this for a fact!
(This comment came from a man of about 60 years.)

I am 80 and have heard some pretty bizarre myths in my lifetime, but that one about the pin-holes in condoms takes the cake. I have heard it before, and

would like to say it is perpetrated by people who want to put their fear of sex into others!
(This was from another, rather better informed, male.)

I am an unequivocal advocate of vasectomy. We have two great kids, and this has dissolved all worry about further pregnancies with a minimum of fuss!

Chapter Two

Relationships

'Love is a many-splendoured thing', as the old love song says. It is not only songs that testify to how in love with love we are. Magazines, movies, soapies, chat shows and casual gossip all rely heavily on the subject of love affairs. Who is doing what to whom? How is such-and-such faring in a relationship? What would I do if I were in her shoes? Everywhere you turn, love is a central theme.

A good proportion of our lives is spent pining for and pursuing Ms or Mr Right, but when our quarry has finally been caught we all too often stop concentrating our attention on our relationship. Consequently, when things start to go wrong — when one partner becomes bored or starts staying late at work to avoid the situation at home, or letting others into intimacies once so fiercely protected — the other partner starts asking why.

This happens because we were never taught anything about taking care of a relationship. Instead, we were led to believe that love took care of everything. Poor old love; we ask it to do the impossible. We go to great lengths in the beginning to understand and consider each other, then ease off at the very time we should be putting in some serious effort. The fact is, even the best of relationships requires a lot of hard work, on the part of both partners, to remain thriving and fulfilling.

If your relationship is good, more often than not your sex life will also be good. As with most rules, there will be exceptions to this, but most of the time it applies. If you make your relationship as exciting, interesting and satisfying as you need it to be, then it will follow that your sex life will also be exciting, interesting and satisfying.

In fact, your sex life is an excellent barometer for checking the state of your relationship. If there are problems, sex is where they will show up first. Many callers on our program started out describing a sexual problem, but it usually emerged that the real problem was within the relationship. For example, a caller might say that he was unable to talk to his wife about changing some part of their lovemaking. In this instance, the real problem is communication, not just sex. We have also had many calls from people saying they had trouble initiating sexual relationships. It usually emerged, however, that they had trouble getting into *any* relationship, and they needed to work on developing worthwhile friendships before rushing into the sexual side of relationships.

Many problems in sexual relationships arise from the fact that the two partners have differing emotional and sexual needs. If these aren't recognised and discussed frankly, further misunderstandings and problems will almost certainly follow. We have dealt fully with this common situation in Chapter 6.

In our answers to the questions from listeners that follow, we discuss many common relationship problems, including:

- how to start a sexual relationship
- how to tell love from infatuation
- what to do if you suspect your partner of infidelity

- how to cope with feelings of insecurity within the relationship
- what to do when a relationship seems to be going wrong
- what to expect from yourself when a relationship has ended.

Question

We have been going out together for a few months and enjoy each other's company immensely, but we haven't had sex yet. I want to, and I am sure he does too, but I just don't know how to start it. Can you advise me?

Answer

This is often a concern for a couple who have kept things friendly and casual at the beginning, but who find it difficult to make the transition to a physical relationship. They have each hung back in case their partner rejects them, and, as a consequence, they have both become increasingly up-tight about the sexual side of their relationship.

It is an ironic situation, because couples who have avoided sex in this way often have the strongest feelings for each other. Their emotions can be almost overwhelming. As well as their passion for each other, they have to cope with an uneasiness about what the other is thinking and feeling, and the anxiety about starting sex. Such intense anxiety and sex don't mix at all well. This is the first thing a couple in this situation must realise.

So the worst thing you could do at this stage would be to rush into it. Having waited this long, you should wait a little longer. You need to discuss your deep feelings for each other, your anxiety and the possibility of having sex. Talking about your feelings to one another like this will shake loose a great deal of that anxiety.

At this point you'll also need to discuss the questions of safe sex and contraception (see Chapter 1).

Once you have paved the way like this and you feel that great blanket of anxiety start to lift, there is no point in further delaying the start of your sex life. However, if you are still a bit dithery about it, try saying to yourself:

'We have now discussed having sex, therefore we need to go ahead with our sexual relationship. The first few times it will probably be disappointing, but with practice we will relax more and get better at it.'

It is most important to recognise and accept the possibility that the first few times together will probably be less than satisfactory.

Before you have intercourse, spend a lot of time relaxing and *slowly* arousing each other. You will be less likely to be disappointed with the whole event if you take plenty of time.

Throughout your relationship make sure you continue to talk about your feelings, keeping the lines of communication open about what you do and do not like about your sex life.

Question

I have been going out with my girlfriend for three months now and I think I love her, but I get this niggling fear that it is only infatuation. How can I tell the difference?

Answer

We wonder how many times this question has been asked in one form or another!

If we are talking about feelings, there is no way to distinguish love from infatuation. They are the same. Psychologists have tried to distinguish between the two by surveying thousands who have claimed to be either 'in love' or 'infatuated'. When asked, people used exactly the same words to describe love as they did to describe infatuation.

Infatuation is nearly always used in the past tense. When a relationship has ended you will find people refer to it as infatuation. Full of the wisdom hindsight brings, they imply that the relationship was doomed from the outset because it was 'only infatuation' and therefore the couple could not have been 'in love'.

In short, it does not matter if you are in love or infatuated, because either brings on exactly the same intense responses: daydreaming about your partner; a rush of anxiety when you see or hear him or her, particularly if you cross paths unexpectedly; wondering what your partner is doing and with whom; extreme highs and at the same time strong doubts about whether the relationship will last; doubts also about your partner's feelings towards you; and a very strong, passionate sexual attraction.

These are the feelings commonly associated with a new relationship and, at this stage of the game, there will be many ups and downs. In the down times, when doubts occur, people sometimes start referring to their new-found love as 'just infatuation', conveniently talking themselves out of it. And they do this to try to avoid being hurt by the other person.

A decidedly healthier approach is to recognise your doubts for what they really are: your uncertainty about the relationship and your partner (a natural thing to have at this stage). Then, every time doubts start nagging away, try saying something like this to offset their negative effect:

'I don't know if this relationship will last and I don't know this new person very well, but I like him/her and I

25

am prepared to try to do something to make sure things are as good as they can possibly be.'

That way you give yourself a real chance to make it work out. As well, you lessen your anxiety about the whole thing by taking the emphasis off what you think your partner thinks and feels, focusing, instead, on what you can do to improve things.

Most relationships begin passionately. Both people have the intense feelings we described earlier and want to see as much of each other as possible. It can be quite a spectacular time in the love affair. The relationship is kept at fever pitch, but eventually things do cool down. They have to. Let's face it, no one could live like that for long. As wonderful as it is, it would cause havoc to the rest of your life. Once the cooling-off process starts, it is the relationship skills both people employ that will keep things bubbling along and make the relationship grow. Love or infatuation (call it what you may) is not enough.

Briefly, you will need to be able to: communicate; spend time together doing fun things you both really enjoy; have an understanding, non-defensive attitude towards your partner; develop confidence in yourself; develop an affectionate, fun — even playful — attitude towards each other; solve major problems that may arise; and develop a comfortable, but interesting, sexual relationship.

If you feel you don't know enough about these skills, refer to the Recommended Reading listed at the back of this book. Practise these skills so that you have them well established before the passion begins to fade.

Question

My husband is having an affair. What should I do?

First you have to speak to your partner about it. However, the subject must be approached very sensitively. Otherwise you will get a defensive reply that could stop any further talk, closing down communication completely. If you accuse a husband, wife, girlfriend or boyfriend of having an affair in an aggressive or threatening way, they will only respond in the same way. No matter how distressed, upset and hurt you feel, a straightforward approach is a must.

It is also important here to put right out of your mind any thoughts of revenge or retaliatory behaviour. They will only stop you acting constructively and calmly.

This does not mean you will feel calm about the situation, because you won't. You will feel bad! Probably as bad as you have felt at any time in your life. But your objective, at this point, is to sort out what is going on and what you both want to do about it.

You can cope with those distressed feelings by saying something like this to yourself:

'I feel really hurt, deceived and upset, but I need to deal with the situation calmly. I will take a deep breath, speak quietly and stick to the point.'

Try not to have this discussion in the heat of the moment. Make a time to speak together when there will be no interruptions from children or other people.

In this discussion, try to establish the correct facts about the situation and express your feelings. While it is essential you handle things calmly, that doesn't mean that you have to hide your feelings from your partner. Maybe you can try something like this for openers:

'I feel upset that you are involved with Jill. I would like to talk about it and also about the implications for our relationship.'

Or, if you don't know definitely that your partner is involved with someone else:

'I am uncertain about your involvement with Jill, but I am suspicious because I saw you together [or whatever has raised the suspicion in your mind], and I would like to discuss it. If you *are* involved I would rather find out and discuss it now than later.'

Be prepared to hear the worst. If your partner confirms your suspicions, it is a good idea to end the conversation right there, because what usually happens is that the shock of such a revelation is so upsetting — no matter how suspicious you were — that things quickly get out of hand.

Have a close friend on standby. Go to him or her and share your distress. Many couples make the mistake of trying to share their hurt and confused feelings with each other at this stage. Unfortunately this just doesn't work. Make it clear by being open with your partner that whatever he or she has done is not acceptable, but express your feelings to someone else.

Now that you know what is going on you will need further discussion to work out what you are going to do about it. If you and your partner decide to stay together, then you will have to work on your relationship. If one person has become involved with someone else, it is usually a sign that the relationship has some flaws. You will need to mend those flaws and you may need some professional help to do so.

We would hazard a guess that in most cases when couples marry or decide on long-term relationships, the last thing they discuss is their attitude to fidelity. It is usually an unstated assumption that they will remain sexually faithful to each other. However, it has now become an issue for you, in a most upsetting way. If you haven't explicitly discussed whether either or both of you believe in fidelity, you will now need to do so. You may both decide to change that unstated assumption, or you may more clearly state that you are not prepared to have sexual partners outside your relationship.

You may have discussed this issue at the beginning and decided you *would* condone other partners, but obviously something has gone wrong if one of you isn't able to cope with the reality. If you *do* decide to allow other partners, either at the outset of the relationship or now that it has become an issue, first make sure that what you have together is working well enough not to be threatened by another relationship. Then spell out clearly the rules and agreements under which you can both see others. This takes a long time and lots of work.

Question

My wife is having an affair. I'm stunned. There was no hint anything was wrong. I found out in a most unfortunate way, after everyone else.

Her excuse is that I was not offering her enough enjoyment. She has been gone three days and when I've tried to contact her, she has been very hostile towards me. Anything I say is met with defensiveness.

The man is much older and therefore has a lot more he can offer her. Is there anything I can do to get her back? Please help me.

Answer

This is perhaps one of the saddest stories. Somewhere along the line, you did not hear the warning bells. As it has only been three days, if you are able to talk calmly with her, she may be willing to work on whatever is wrong. However, her hostility and defensiveness are not a good sign.

Right now you are feeling so distressed, hurt and deceived that it is difficult to think things through clearly. But a little later on, you must challenge those ideas that she left because he was older, or had better materialistic offerings, or even was more skilled sexually.

Those are rarely the reasons that a person leaves. She was probably giving you signs that things were wrong, but never clearly stating her case. Or she may have tried and you were not receptive. When she felt she could bear the situation no longer she just left, without giving either of you the chance to work things out. Now, unfortunately, it may be too late. But it is still important to work out the 'why' of what has happened — both for your peace of mind, and for future relationships. (See also the answer to the previous question.)

Question

I am in a very good relationship — it is the best I have had — but I am frightened it will not last. What should I do?

Answer

Fear or anxiety that a relationship will not last is enough to cause problems, or even the downfall of that relationship. Anxiety causes road-blocks in relationships. It can block anything from good communication to good sex.

You would be hard-pushed to prevent or get rid of these feelings, because they occur spontaneously and quite naturally. However, you can stop them getting out of control — from going over the top. When you find yourself feeling insecure and fearing that the relationship won't last, take a deep breath and relax. Don't fight your uncertainty. If you do, you will only make yourself feel worse. Go with the bad feeling, but then say something reassuring to yourself like:

'I feel really insecure at the moment, but if I just wait a

while, this feeling will pass and I will be able to carry on.'

Then count to ten and make yourself think or do something else. DON'T continue to worry about your partner.

If, however, you feel it is reasonable to say something about your partner's behaviour, then add this to your statement:

'I think it's reasonable to say something about this. I will wait for an opportunity to state my feelings calmly.'

It is impossible to say when you should tell someone how you feel about their behaviour, and when you should cope with your own feelings. It isn't always right to say something, but neither is it always right to try and cope yourself; somewhere in the middle is about right.

When to speak up and when to keep quiet are skills you will perfect the more you practise. If you *are* prepared to practise you will get more and more of a feel for what to do, and when to do it. Make sure you express your feelings in a quiet, straightforward manner and don't allow the situation to deteriorate. End the discussion before you argue, if that looks likely. Then come back to it later when you are both calmer.

While you are learning to make all these changes in yourself, let your partner know what is on your mind. Explain that you are anxious at times about the relationship, that it is very good and you don't want to lose it, but that at times this frightens you. Your partner will be able to understand your behaviour better if you explain yourself.

Question

My husband always wants to have sex, and doesn't respect my point of view when I say no. Should I leave him?

To leave or not to leave. We will deal with that in a moment. Often when this problem occurs it can be sorted out by discovering why the partner wants so much sex. Rarely do people want sex just for erotic gratification. There are other reasons, many of which can be fulfilled in ways other than having intercourse.

It could be that your partner is after affection, or he could be pressuring you into sex because he wants to spend more time with you. Maybe he doesn't feel he is attractive to you any more, and sex reassures him that he is. He could be demanding sex all the time simply because he wants to feel close to you. (See also Chapter 6.) Once it is clear why one partner wants more sex than the other, you can set about finding the appropriate ways to satisfy those needs.

If, however, your partner refuses point-blank to discuss the problem, he is showing a lack of goodwill, trust and faith in your relationship.

You ask if you should leave him. This is something you will have to decide for yourself. What one person likes or is prepared to accept in a relationship may not be acceptable to another. The bottom line, however, is that if you feel unhappy you need to do something.

At this stage, it would be a good idea to get some counselling together. If your partner refuses, all you will get out of any sessions on your own is a clear understanding of why the relationship is not working. While this can be helpful, it doesn't solve your problems.

If your partner is prepared to work on what is wrong, and goes along with you to see a counsellor, then you are a good way towards solving your problems. With some effort and time you will be back on the road with a more solid, enjoyable and rewarding relationship.

We can't emphasise enough how important it is that you see a counsellor who has the right training (see

Support Organisations). And beware of counselling that offers you relationship therapy with only one of you present. A relationship takes two.

Question

My relationship ended twelve months ago, and I don't seem to be coping with separation. I haven't been able to meet anyone else. Can you advise me?

Answer

It's an advantage *not* to have become involved with someone else for this period of time after the end of your last relationship. Twelve months is ideal. But now is the time to begin meeting new people and getting into a new relationship. Here is the reason.

Most people seem to recognise that when they initially separate, they feel bad. They have to leave a familiar situation and face the unknown. They also have to begin to see themselves as single, make new friends, live in new circumstances — probably with a drop in income — and so on.

However, many people don't seem to realise how long it takes to adjust to all these changes. It's quite usual for it to take from six to twelve months for you to start feeling anything like your old self again. In some cases it will take even longer. In this time all you can expect of yourself is to gradually learn to adjust to your new way of life. Many make the mistake of trying to start a new relationship immediately, while they are still learning to cope with ending the old one.

People who are particularly vulnerable are those who have left one relationship for another. Not realising what an enormous strain it is to end a partnership, they pile more pressure on themselves by immediately committing themselves to someone else. Often this all has a very bad effect on the new relationship, and things go from bad to worse.

It is better to successfully end one, wait a year — or even more if you need to — then consider getting involved again. This, of course, doesn't mean you can't develop friendships in the meantime, or go out and meet new people. Simply give yourself time to get over your previous long-term relationship before starting another.

Get involved with a group of people doing something you really enjoy. It could be by taking up a hobby or joining classes at your local Council of Adult Education. Don't try going to discos or pubs. You will find it very difficult to meet people and make friends at these places at the best of times. Join your group with a view to just making friends, and not specifically to find a partner. You will scare off potential friends if your approach is a heavy one, first up.

Once you have established friendships, then start going out with some people you like. Keep things casual at first, and don't become involved too fast. Don't grab at the first possible relationship. Take plenty of time, and make sure you meet lots of new people. However, don't overdo the waiting. You will sense the correct time to plunge in. But plunge gradually! As time goes by, bit-by-bit, increase your involvement and commitment.

If at any stage you have trouble coping with separation, whether it's at the beginning, when you are distressed and upset, or later, when you are depressed and unhappy with your life, don't hesitate to seek advice and counselling. You could find that one or two sessions help you back on your feet, whereas, had you let it go, you could have been on the wrong track for a long time. In the process, you could have made yourself very unhappy.

Chapter Three

Orgasm

Do I experience orgasm?
Should I experience orgasm?
Does it matter who reaches orgasm first?
What if I don't have an orgasm?
What would my partner think if I didn't have an orgasm?
Should I tell my boyfriend I can't have an orgasm?
Should I say I'm faking it?

On and on go the questions about orgasm! More often than not we think of orgasm as a mystical process that usually occurs for men, and occurs only sometimes for women. There is very little understanding of what is really involved, why it happens.

In physical terms, orgasm is the contraction of the muscles surrounding the penis and vagina. These contractions are about 0.8 seconds apart at first, then taper off. The first ones will be very intense and are often associated with a sense of fainting or losing awareness of oneself. The following contractions are less intense, but a sense of deep relaxation follows.

It is difficult to describe how it feels to have an orgasm. The sensations vary from person to person, and from time to time for the one person. However, orgasms are surprisingly alike for both men and women. Despite the obvious differences, the male's penis and the female's clitoris are similar parts of the body.

Because orgasm is an automatic process it is possible for it to occur without us having to understand any of the underlying physical reactions. What *is* necessary, however, is to know how to become *sufficiently aroused* so that orgasm can occur.

Often, the questions we have been asked on radio indicate that people don't understand orgasm happens automatically, that all you have to work on is the arousal!

The questions reflect a belief that you can *control* orgasm and make it happen. This is quite simply not the case. All you can do is set up the circumstances to give you the best possible chance of having an orgasm.

Today, we demand instant answers to problems, and we are also accustomed to controlling our environment. But, like the weather, orgasms are out of our direct control — and we find this very hard to accept. But we have to learn to accept it. In other words, there is no instant answer to the question, 'Why don't I have an orgasm?'.

It is foreign for us to think of our body as something that works *with* us and not *for* us, as something that we have to respect, learn to understand and attend and respond to. We are more likely to think it should obey us, jump at our every command. But it doesn't, and this makes us very upset. You could honestly say that problems with orgasms can occur when we think too much!

The following is a simple explanation of why you should try to go onto 'automatic' at the point of orgasm. There is an automatic part of the nervous system that is not under conscious control. The thinking part of your brain can influence this automatic part, but it can't make it respond in a particular way. Therefore, you have to learn to *allow* the automatic part of your brain and nervous system to respond to sexual stimulation, working *with* it, and not *against* it.

This process is fundamental to being able to have an

orgasm. Often people who aren't able to have an orgasm are interfering with their automatic process by thinking too much.

Many books about sex go into great detail about the physical process of orgasm, describing at length the physiological changes that take place in the body during climax, but ignoring the most important aspect: how to reach high levels of arousal and orgasm.

The physical information is certainly interesting, but it's about as helpful as being told what is going to happen in your digestive system to a piece of luscious chocolate cake, when all you wanted to do was to eat and enjoy it. It's not necessary. Therefore, we will only briefly describe the physical process. There are more detailed descriptions in some of the books listed under Recommended Reading at the back of this book.

PHYSIOLOGICAL CHANGES

Basically, there are two physiological responses that occur during arousal and the involuntary climax: the flow of blood into tissues, particularly those surrounding the genitals and pelvic area; and the increase in muscle tension all over the body.

In men, this in-flow of blood produces the erection of the penis, and in women, the swelling of the clitoris and the darkening, swelling and lubrication of the vagina. The muscle tension, in both men and women, increases arousal to the point of orgasm. At this point, in both sexes, the muscle tissue surrounding the genitals contracts at regular intervals and this is what produces the orgasm. This in turn leads to ejaculation for men. After that there is a gradual out-flow of blood from the genital area and, in both sexes, these areas return to their pre-arousal state.

Other general physical symptoms you might experience

during arousal include flushing of the skin, temperature changes due to the in-flow of blood, and perspiration caused by the physical activity and increased heat of the body. High levels of sexual tension can also lead to an increase in pulse rate which, at the point of orgasm, can be very high indeed. Blood pressure also registers an increase and the breathing rate goes up, not, as you might imagine, purely in response to the physical activity, but specifically in response to sexual arousal.

As we have already said, most of these physical responses are *not* under control of the thinking part of the brain, they are taken care of by the automatic part. Consequently, all you have to do is relax and let things happen. Your only job is to make sure you and your partner are sufficiently aroused. And don't 'think' yourself out of an orgasm!

Question

I have been married for one year and still haven't had an orgasm. I hadn't had any other sex partners before my husband. He is very disappointed that I haven't been able to climax. Is there something wrong with me?

Answer

Unfortunately, it seems that women still don't get the opportunity or encouragement to explore their sexual feelings as they are growing up, in the way a man does. Then when they get into an adult sexual relationship, they find it hard to respond physically to sexual stimulation because they have not had any practice.

There is certainly nothing wrong with you, but if you don't sort it out now it could lead to some future sexual difficulties. For example, sex will become less and less interesting for you if all you are getting out of it is emotional pleasure, not sexual pleasure.

Some women channel their sexual energy into other non-sexual activities. Then they get surprised and upset when a man 'wants to have sex all the time'. But why wouldn't he? After all, he *is* getting emotional and sexual pleasure from it.

This problem really magnifies as the relationship gets older and the passion and intensity of feeling disappear from the sexual side of it, because when passion cools off and the sex act has not grown (as it will not have done if only one is being physically satisfied), both partners are likely to find other ways to fulfil their need for intimacy in the relationship.

It's really desirable that when a couple have sex they both feel interested in what they are doing, and enjoy it. This will usually happen only when both are able to, at times, reach a climax during sex. They don't have to climax every time, but they need to know that they can climax when they want to.

Therefore, it is worth developing your own sexuality to a level where you can climax whenever you want to. And to reach this level a woman has to begin to explore her sexuality through a program of masturbation (see also Chapter 4). Until she can climax on her own, it will be very difficult for her to climax with her partner. Masturbation will teach her how. As part of this masturbation program, she will need to train her head to respond sexually.

As we have already explained, the physical process of orgasm will occur automatically, but your head has to *allow* it to happen. Thinking can very easily stop the physical process at the point of orgasm. 'Don't think, feel' would be a good motto for you to adopt. To do this you must focus your attention on the physical sensations in your body, *not thinking*, just focusing. You may find it helps if you maintain an erotic fantasy in your head. If

39

you are just learning to masturbate, you will probably do better if you use a fantasy, as your focusing skills will not be sufficiently developed. What can happen is that you start talking to yourself in your head, and, even if these thoughts are positive — such as, 'This is nice' — they will still interfere with your sexual arousal. Focusing attention has nothing to do with thinking.

Expect it to take you quite a while to learn how to focus attention and not think. It will also take a lot of practice, practice that will, no doubt, be frustrating at times, but in the end well worth it.

During this time of learning, make sure you continue to have sex with your partner. Then, once you can achieve orgasm easily by yourself, include him. Tell him what you have discovered about yourself.

Treat your masturbation program as something you are doing to improve your lovemaking technique — don't worry about how long it takes — and continue to enjoy your sexual relationship. Sex is more than orgasm.

Question

I'm not sure if I've had an orgasm. What does it feel like?

Answer

At the risk of being maddening, we could answer by saying, 'If you've had one you'd know!', the reason being that orgasm is usually a very intense feeling, so that anyone who is in doubt about having had one, probably has not.

However, we should bear in mind that one individual's orgasmic feeling could be as different from the next person's as chalk and cheese. The sensation will even vary from time to time for the one person.

Many have attempted to describe how it feels to have an orgasm, but descriptions probably only confuse a person who is uncertain about having had one. For the inexperienced it is easy to confuse arousal with orgasm. When they describe what they think might be orgasm, they are describing what are really very high levels of arousal.

Arousal is the stage just before the contractions of orgasm happen. If you are only getting to this stage, the next time it happens ask your partner to continue whatever he has been doing that is bringing on your highly aroused state. Then you must allow yourself to be swept along by these feelings — remember, 'Don't think, feel' — and let orgasm happen.

If this doesn't work, you may have to go through a masturbation program (described in answer to the previous question). Try to explore the things that really turn you on and practise being swept along until you are overwhelmed by how you feel, rather than monitor in your head whether or not you are having an orgasm.

If you feel slightly on edge, irritable or downright cross after sex, then it is probable that you have reached a high level of arousal and not orgasm. Rather than reading about the sensations of orgasm and how they should feel, it is better to try to achieve them. Practise with your partner or with masturbation, as described above.

Question

I can reach an orgasm when I masturbate, but just can't make the grade with my boyfriend. Why is this?

Answer

Questions like this usually come from women. There are a few good reasons why women can have trouble having orgasms during lovemaking with a partner.

It could be that both she and her partner expect her to experience orgasm through intercourse. Some women certainly can do this, but most need direct stimulation of the clitoris to achieve orgasm.

When a woman masturbates, contrary to popular belief, she reaches orgasm by directly stimulating her clitoris. (The popular misconception is that she needs something in her vagina to reach a climax.) A woman does not reach orgasm because she has inserted objects into her vagina during masturbation. She may like the feel of something in her vagina, but that is not what gives her the orgasm. Therefore, during lovemaking a woman needs direct clitoral stimulation, either during intercourse, with the man using his hand, or before or after intercourse. Stimulation can be manual or oral before or after intercourse.

A woman can learn to have an orgasm during intercourse, but she needs the help of her partner. He will need to manually stimulate her clitoris while she is having intercourse, then, at the point of orgasm, stop the clitoral stimulation and continue with just the intercourse. The process has to be repeated over and over again until the woman has an orgasm. It can be tiresome and difficult, but if you are keen, give it a go. A small warning: don't get your hopes up too high because it may not work due to its tiresome nature. Better to have an attitude of 'Let's just try and see what happens'.

The other reason that a woman may not be able to achieve orgasm during sex with a partner is because she has been using a masturbation technique that is impossible to incorporate into sex with a partner. One such technique involves a woman lying on her tummy and masturbating by rubbing herself up and down on a pillow, with her legs closed together very tightly. This is a popular form of masturbation for women, but one in which it would obviously be difficult, if not impossible, to involve a partner.

There is also the situation where a woman has one way, and one way only, in which she can reach orgasm, so that unless the partner can repeat the process exactly, it is impossible for her to achieve orgasm with him.

With both these problems the woman has to practise a wider variety of masturbation techniques to enable her to have an orgasm in a number of different situations, with a number of different positions and types of stimulation. Once she discovers these herself, through masturbation, it will be fairly easy to involve her partner.

Both men and women can have trouble reaching orgasm with a partner if they have a relationship problem. Doubts, fears or uncertainties about their relationship are enough to keep an orgasm at bay. If they have been arguing or feel antagonistic towards each other, then either one or both of them may have trouble relaxing enough to reach orgasm during sex. If this happens, they need to try to work out what their problem is and discuss quietly and calmly why they feel upset and hurt (see also Chapter 6).

Sometimes the bad feelings may be associated with the sexual relationship. One of the partners may do something that annoys the other. Again, they need to calmly and quietly discuss the problem — but definitely not at the time they are having sex. Just the process of trying to understand each other's point of view can make a couple feel closer to each other. However, that is not enough. They have to follow it through until they have it sorted out.

If the problem is bigger than both of you, and you have no luck solving it, the worst thing you could do is ignore it, hoping it will go away. It won't. Get some professional help from a clinical psychologist. Don't be apprehensive about this, because it is no big deal. If you choose one carefully, as we discussed in our Introduction, you will find that one or two sessions should put you back on the right path. It's best to do this at an early stage, before the problem gets worse.

Finally, people can have trouble reaching orgasm if they have had a very repressive sexual upbringing. The anxiety associated with sex for these people is so great that they have trouble relaxing, letting go and allowing the orgasm to happen. It is a similar problem for those who were sexually abused as children. They have the same trouble letting go in a sexual relationship. Either of these problems requires professional help.

Question

We want to reach orgasm together, but no matter how hard we try, we can't do it. Is there anything wrong with this?

Answer

How sad a question like this is! A couple has what seems in all ways to be a good sexual relationship and they start doubting whether it is 'right' because one of them heard or read somewhere that climaxes should be simultaneous. This is really crazy!

Despite the impression you may get from popular literature or lightweight articles in magazines, or from what you see in movies, it is extremely rare — almost impossible — for a couple to have an orgasm at the same time. It is more good luck than anything else if it happens — a bit like winning the lottery. The reason is quite simple: usually while one partner is concentrating on stimulating the other, it is very hard to pay enough attention to himself or herself to reach orgasm.

On the other hand, if you get lucky and reach orgasm together, there is nothing wrong with that! But there is no need to spend time trying to attain this arbitrary goal, particularly if you are both satisfied with your sexual relationship the way it is. Sex is for enjoyment and togetherness, not for attaining records or goals.

Question

My wife gets very wet when she comes. If I haven't had an orgasm, it makes it very difficult to remain inside her. Is there something medically wrong with her?

Answer

The amount of lubrication women produce varies. It also varies in the one woman in accordance with the level of arousal reached. It is very unlikely that she has something medically wrong with her. You may have to achieve orgasm through stimulation other than intercourse on these occasions — such as oral sex or masturbation.

Question

Do men fake orgasm?

Answer

One of the helpful things about discussing sex with people on radio was that it gave the scientific data and surveys a human face. It was possible to get a real idea of what happened in people's sex lives.

In a way we had our own constant mini-survey going all the time. Not that it had any scientific validity, but it helped us to give a more rounded-out answer to a question like this.

Yes, men do fake orgasm. Many of the men who spoke with us reported faking the big 'O'. Even more interesting was their reason — the very reason that women give for faking it: 'I don't want to disappoint my partner'.

Women, it has been generally assumed, make out they have an orgasm because they don't want to upset, hurt or lose their partner. They put on a sexual performance. According to our experience, men also do the same thing for exactly the same reasons.

Instead of hopping on that merry-go-round of trying to guess what our partner feels, then responding the way we assume they want us to, life would be so much easier if we voiced how we felt and what we wanted in an understanding way.

Another reason for faking orgasm, which men were willing to give anonymously on radio, was that sometimes in the middle of sex their interest just evaporated, and they could not get it back. And then there were the times when they had not been interested from the beginning. Instead of perhaps saying 'Let's just cuddle', 'Let's watch TV', or 'Let's go out', they said yes to sex they didn't feel like.

The main problem with taking this short-cut approach is that in the long term, it leads to doubts and resentment. Even though your partner has not forced you to have sex, you have been reluctant to ask for what you want. And in failing to do that you create a certain amount of resentment and uncertainty for yourself. If it happens very often in a relationship it leads to a long-standing backlog of negative feelings with which it becomes increasingly difficult to deal.

It is far better to upset a partner in the short term (assuming that this is how she will react to your honesty) than to allow resentments to build up that eventually destroy the relationship.

Question

Do men have more than one orgasm at a time? I've heard they can have multiple orgasms the way some women can.

Answer

It has been widely known for a number of years that some women can have repeated orgasms with little time between each climax, but it was generally believed that men needed a much longer period between each climax. Although there was wide variation in the length of time men needed, twenty minutes to half an hour was the accepted average.

This belief about men seems to have come from the not unreasonable association between orgasm and ejaculation. Usually ejaculation and orgasm happen together, but men don't necessarily have to ejaculate to have an orgasm.

Only recently have men reported that after they ejaculate the first time, if their partner continues to stimulate them, they can go on to have multiple orgasms without ejaculation. Physiologically, this is possible because orgasm happens due to the muscles in the genital area — around the base of the penis — contracting. There is no need to ejaculate to reach orgasm.

When we introduced male multiple orgasms as a subject on our radio program we had a fabulous response from men eager to relate their experiences. Quite a number of them said they had been having multiple orgasms for many years. However, to date there is no scientific evidence to support this phenomenon.

During my eighteen-year marriage I climaxed only twice! Since I've been widowed I've been to a clinical psychologist and have learned to climax on my own. I have also had two relationships in that time. The last one was terrific sexually. I found my G-spot and had no trouble at all with orgasm.

The problem is that with my present partner I have returned to life without orgasms!

Hard as he tries, he can't find my G-spot. I have a prolapse of the womb which might be covering my G-spot. The only way I have orgasm now is with a lot of hard work on my part stimulating my clitoris.

I've never yet met a woman who can have an orgasm when I want her to. Intercourse should last for a long time, because the lead-up to it is a wonderful state to be in. But where I can go on and on and on, women seem to get bored with it. It can also hurt a woman, so I have to stop.

I'm 19, have been in a relationship for two years, but can't reach orgasm. I have no trouble when I masturbate, but with my girlfriend it is just not happening.

I concentrate very hard on fantasising when we have sex, but even that is difficult because I get so tense about having an orgasm that my concentration just goes out the window. She is happy with sex, but I think that is because I haven't told her I don't come. I make out I do.

I'm ringing for my wife who has trouble having an orgasm. We certainly can't achieve it for her during intercourse, nor can we make it work when I use my hand or tongue.

I have never reached orgasm with my present partner, and it is embarrassing me to death. Is it because I have never masturbated? The reason I haven't is that I find the idea objectionable. I thought I was having orgasms with my husband, but as I've got older and learned more about sex I've come to the conclusion that all I had was a fairly high state of arousal.

Chapter Four

Masturbation

Almost no other subject that we introduced on radio uncovered as much unnecessary guilt, ignorance or general discomfort as masturbation.

To know how to masturbate and to do so are essential parts of our sexual well-being, but we seem to have a real block about accepting this. The word itself puts up walls. Masturbation is a clumsy-sounding word; the alternative, 'autoeroticism', is not much better.

However, it is very common behaviour, although almost no one will talk about it or admit to doing it. This reticence is understandable because, for many years, masturbation was referred to in a very negative way. Even if we no longer believe the old wives' tales about the harmful effects of masturbation, very few of us are able to talk comfortably about its positive effects.

During the last ten years or so, there has been an increased awareness by professionals involved in helping people with sexual problems that masturbation is useful and necessary in some treatment programs (see also Chapter 3). But even this level of acceptance doesn't mean that it has become something that is openly discussed and encouraged.

Masturbation is still seen as very much a male-oriented activity. Our society generally accepts, or turns a blind eye to, young boys exploring their genitals, but young girls are still given the impression that to touch *their* genitals is a very bad thing. We heap moral 'wrongs' on it for females, but silently condone it for males.

Some optimistic souls may say a change in attitude is slowly occurring. But very few parents would encourage this activity or recognise it as a positive sexual development — particularly for their daughters.

If we could view masturbation quite simply as something that occurs in most human beings as part of their sexuality, there would be no need to make a huge fuss about it, either way. It could be treated very matter-of-factly, as something that everyone has the right to pursue in private. It could also be seen as a healthy part of sexual development that enabled people to learn more about their own sexuality, and to express that sexuality in a harmless way when they didn't have an appropriate partner. There would be no need for guilt or doubts to arise about using masturbation as an outlet for sexual expression; it could be seen as just another part of living.

Unfortunately, it is rarely viewed like this. As a result, masturbation is used inappropriately or not at all, so many problems have become associated with it. We will discuss these later.

Let's first define masturbation. Generally, it's considered to be self-stimulation to the point of orgasm. This stimulation can happen in many ways. Some women can masturbate to orgasm through stimulation of their nipples alone, some report being able to reach orgasm using only sexual fantasies, while others achieve it through muscle tension by crossing their legs. Most of the time, however, masturbation is the hand-manipulation of the genitals, or friction caused by rubbing against something. Usually this physical stimulation is accompanied by an erotic fantasy.

The subject of the erotic fantasy can be important. If

you masturbate to the same particular fantasy each time, you will feel more and more sexually attracted to that one particular type of stimulation. The pleasurable, intense feelings of orgasm are very powerful and so anything associated with them may become increasingly attractive to you.

Through masturbation you can learn to develop good, healthy sexual behaviour. Unfortunately, you could also develop sexual tendencies that could cause future problems, depending on the fantasy involved.

There has always been some controversy about sexual fantasies. Some people believe that if you fantasise about a sexual situation, you may be tempted to act it out. Others argue that fantasies have no basis in reality, and that just because someone fantasises about something doesn't mean he or she would actually do it.

Both schools of thought have some truth; it all depends on the individual involved. Many people, who use the most outrageous sexual fantasies, would never be tempted to act them out. Others, however, who fantasise about illegal sexual behaviour, eventually act out their fantasies in real life.

The key to the distinction between the two groups is probably the frequency of the fantasy. If it is constant and never varies, then the person is possibly at risk of acting it out in real life. This needn't be a bad thing if the sexual behaviour in the fantasy is acceptable. It is when the sexual behaviour is *not* acceptable in our society — that is, when, like child molestation, it is illegal — that there may be problems.

I masturbate three or four times a week. Is that normal?

There is no such thing as 'normal'. Increased access to statistics and information seems to have proportionately increased people's self-consciousness about 'measuring up to the facts'. The so-called 'facts and figures' are often very misleading, especially if the reader has no understanding of statistics. A good example is the oft-quoted 'married couples have sex twice a week' type of data.

This average is made up of couples who are newlyweds and may have sex three times every day as well as couples who have longer-standing relationships and have sex once every three weeks or, if they are on holidays or both feeling good, more frequently. The magic figure 'twice a week' means absolutely nothing and has nothing to do with what people, as individuals, do in their sex lives.

So with masturbation, as with other forms of sexual behaviour, there is no such thing as 'normal'. However, there are a few guidelines to bear in mind.

- When you masturbate make sure you do so in an appropriate place, at an appropriate time.
- Don't masturbate just because you are feeling bad.
- Make sure it is not interfering with other day-to-day activities in your life.
- Make sure you are not masturbating to avoid having sex with a partner.

Remember, there are no harmful side-effects to masturbation. You will not hurt yourself physically if you are using your hand to masturbate. You may if you use certain objects, but this is a matter of common sense. You can't make yourself infertile or impotent by masturbating. And, heaven forbid, it *won't* cause hair to grow on your hands, nor will it give you acne!

If you still feel bad about masturbating you have probably been influenced by the negative attitudes that still abound on the subject. Their effect has been to make you feel uncomfortable about it, to feel that it's morally wrong to masturbate. If this is the case, you need to reassure yourself. You could do so by saying something like this to yourself:

'It's okay to masturbate as long as I am doing it for sexual pleasure. It's a good way to express myself sexually. There's no point in making myself upset about it.'

If you keep feeling guilty or bad, it is possible to turn masturbation into an obsessive habit. It's like anything you try hard not to do — you wind up fighting yourself and aggravating the problem. You will be better off learning to accept the fact that you masturbate. It's doing no one any harm. Once you feel more relaxed and accepting of your behaviour the obsession will disappear. You will then be free to masturbate when you feel aroused, and at other times, forget about it.

The only other thing you need to consider seriously, if you are masturbating frequently, is that your fantasies are appropriate (that is, that they don't focus on illegal behaviour).

Question

I have used a vibrator during masturbation for some time now. It gives me deep, multiple orgasms. The problem is that when I'm with a man neither his tongue nor his fingers, nor intercourse, can give me anything like the intense feelings I experience with the vibrator. What can I do?

Answer

This is a common complaint from women who have practised having an orgasm with a vibrator. Unfortunately, a man's hand or tongue is never going to be as powerful as an electric or battery-operated vibrator. By using a vibrator this way, you are letting yourself become accustomed to this one type of touch and now need that strength every time to get the same results.

A lot of women find it helpful to start off with a vibrator just to learn how to achieve orgasm. However, it is strongly recommended that, having learnt, you gradually become less dependent on it. The best way to do this is to have one with controls that you can turn down further and further each time. The next step is to masturbate with your fingers, using the vibrator on top of your fingers — the aim being to gradually return to using your fingers to masturbate. This will make it much easier to incorporate your arousal and orgasm needs in a sexual relationship with your partner.

While the effect may not be as intense, it will be much more acceptable than including the vibrator in your sexual relationship with your partner.

It may take you some time to achieve orgasm, but you will learn how to reach that point quicker the more practice you have.

Question

I can't reach ejaculation when I masturbate. As a result I seem to swell up in the genital area. I have changed the way I masturbate in the last two months, for convenience more than anything else.

Since I was a child I have masturbated by lying on my erection and wriggling around on top of it. That way I could, and still can, ejaculate. However, now that I have tried to masturbate using my hand, nothing more than high arousal is happening. Why is this?

Answer

Two or three months is not long enough to change such an entrenched habit. Keep persevering with the help of some appropriate reading matter on masturbation (see Recommended Reading).

Question

I masturbate four or five times a day. How can I stop?

Answer

Listeners may have thought this was a hoax call, or someone boasting about his sexual potential. However, obsessive masturbation is a genuine problem, and a very disruptive one at that. With such behaviour a person has to go to all sorts of lengths to go through the ritual. Sometimes this involves rushing to the lavatory or somewhere private, frequently upsetting social and work activities.

Obviously, when masturbation has reached this point there is something wrong and the person needs professional help. Generally, people who are masturbating often enough to interfere with other aspects of their life, are doing it to cope with some problem. It's not uncommon to find someone who is unemployed, bored and disheartened, masturbating frequently. Anxiety and tension about work or social situations can also be the underlying reasons someone is doing this.

In such cases, masturbation is not the real problem. It's just the symptom of a more general life problem. Under these circumstances, it's best to get professional help so the real problem can be identified and advice given to help solve it.

Question

How should I help my children when they want information about masturbation?

Answer

There are some good books that explain developing sexuality and, as part of that topic, discuss masturbation (see Recommended Reading). Even if your child is very young you will find books appropriate to his or her age. Read one of these books aloud to your children and, as part of the reading process, discuss masturbation.

You don't have to 'sell' it to your children because they explore and touch their genitals from a very early age. All you need to do is be understanding of this behaviour and explain that it must occur in private, not in front of other people, and not in public places. Generally, if children haven't been punished for exploring and touching themselves, they will gradually find out about masturbation for themselves. The books and discussion with adults can help them understand this behaviour and recognise that it's part of their growing up.

If the children are older, a large part of their sex education will have already occurred, the bulk of it probably indirectly. Long ago they will have picked up your attitude towards sexuality, nudity, exploring or touching of genitals, affection and a whole range of other sex-related issues that happen at home. If you feel you would like to help them improve upon this knowledge, then once again you could buy some of the books, appropriate to their age group, which are listed under Recommended Reading.

You could also encourage them to talk to you about anything of which they are not certain. Don't push them to do this; rather let them know that you are willing and able to discuss things whenever they wish to raise the subject. It's better to let older children make the first move to talk. You certainly won't be able to *make* them discuss anything.

They may have trouble talking to you at first. However, once you have provided them with some facts they might relax, trust your knowledge and, in turn, learn to feel more comfortable with you. Then the path will be clear for them to learn to feel more comfortable with their own sexuality and with masturbation.

Question

How do I stop my 6-year-old son masturbating in public?

Answer

Introduce talk about genitals as soon as possible. He would have been exploring his body virtually since birth, so it should not be hard to find a way to do this. Don't make it a sit-down 'let's talk about sex, son', type of discussion. Keep it like any other general discussion that occurs in the home. Usually, parents find the easiest way to do this is to introduce some books — appropriate to a child's age — that discuss masturbation and growing up. *Where Did I Come From?* by Peter Mayle (see Recommended Reading) is one of the best. You will find others in good bookshops.

Controlling *where* he does it is important. A simple explanation, such as it is a private thing and must be done in his room or when other people are not present, is usually sufficient.

Question

I've never masturbated, and I guess it is no coincidence that orgasm escapes me. I can be aroused, but that is as far as it ever goes, which always leaves me frustrated. I feel I have missed out by not masturbating. However, I would give it a go, if only I knew how.

Answer

It is very much a learning experience. Some reading matter, such as *Becoming Orgasmic* by J. Heiman, L. Lo Piccolo and J. Lo Piccolo (see Recommended Reading), will set you on the right path. Don't regret too deeply what you have missed out on; rather realise that you are in the same boat as a lot of other people. Knowing that you are not the only one can have a positive effect. Once you have discovered what stimulates you, you can then set about teaching your partner.

Question

After sex with my wife, I have to get up, go to the bathroom and masturbate. Sex does not fully satisfy me. I think about my wife when I'm doing this, but I guess it happens two times out of three that we make love. Is there any harm in this?

Answer

Not at all. In fact you are doing your wife a favour by thinking of her when you masturbate, because you reinforce interest in the person you fantasise about when you masturbate.

Question

Medication for diabetes stops me ejaculating when I masturbate. I reach orgasm, but there is no semen. Can you advise me?

Answer

See your doctor and explain everything. Different medications have different effects and only he or she will be able to tell you if the lack of ejaculation is due to the medication, the disease or some other disorder. While it is quite normal to achieve orgasm without ejaculation, in your case it is not something you should accept without question.

Question

My boyfriend gets me to watch him masturbate so that I'll know how to handle him. However, I still haven't quite got the right touch. I am unable to bring him to orgasm. Any suggestions?

Answer

Watching can help, but try putting your hand over his as he masturbates to get the rhythm right. This will also help with pressure and will show just where on his penis he likes to be touched.

Question

I don't have sex with my wife any more because I prefer to masturbate. I fantasise about schoolgirls when I do this. My wife doesn't know this. I'm sure

she thinks the lack of sex in our lives is because of my age. I'm 59. Is my behaviour normal?

Answer

You are in a very dangerous situation. If you have not approached schoolgirls for sex by now the time will come when you do if you continue to use only this fantasy when you masturbate. For everyone's sake, you must seek some professional counselling help.

Question

I masturbate so often that I think I have lowered my sperm count. Can this happen to a 15-year-old?

Answer

It would be very unlikely.

Question

Masturbation is a good standby for me in between girlfriends. I'm sure I'm not using it just because I'm bored, because when a new woman comes along I don't do it nearly as much. I'm employed and have sporting interests. Am I okay?

Answer

Of course you are, from what you say. Sounds perfect. The danger is when people replace those healthy normal pursuits of relationships, sport and work, etc. with masturbation.

I'm friendly with a fair few girls who are friends of my mates, but I can't find a girlfriend. I think it is because I'm very overweight. Trouble is the more miserable I get about this, the more I eat. As I get no sex I pull myself off when I see good-looking girls. I do it in private. I'm 17.

My family is a Christian one. I believe in God, go to church with them, etc., but this is one of the reasons I have an awful guilt about masturbation. I know I shouldn't, but I do it quite often. I think most of the other guys at school do it and I try to tell myself it is normal — or at least I shouldn't be so guilty about it — but nothing works. I think I am turning to masturbation more and more because of teasing from friends about not having a girlfriend. I've tried to cut down on it by keeping busy with sport and study, but this gives only temporary relief.

I'm 70 AND I still get erections although I don't have a partner. I find the only thing to do is to masturbate, otherwise it hurts me. Of course, I'm not complaining. I'm just relating my experience.

In genital touching when my wife masturbates me, she is too firm. I find that I get aroused and come long before she does. Sex is difficult for me to talk about with her, or anyone for that matter. I don't know how to say it is too much for me. I also don't know how to get us both to the same point at the same time. She gets a lot of pleasure out of the masturbation, and always wants to finish with an orgasm. My drive just disappears after I come.

**I find that I get the best stimulation when I mastur-
bate by not directly stimulating my clitoris. If I rub
and gently pull the inner lips of my vagina, it gives
enough indirect movement to my clitoris to make me
reach orgasm. Anything more than that is just too
sensitive for me. In fact it hurts my clitoris.**

Chapter Five

The Penis

Over the years we have had so many calls from men who are desperately worried about the appearance or functioning of their penis that we have included a whole chapter on the subject.

Basically, there are long ones and short ones, fat ones and skinny ones, ones that stick straight up and ones that hang down. Penises are as individual as the noses on our faces. They are also the cause of the greatest joy — for obvious reasons — and, as we have seen, the greatest anxiety.

The penis causes men so much worry partly because it plays such an important role in sex, and partly because it is not under conscious control. So when a man would like to appear sexually aroused, he can't just say to himself, 'Now I will get an erection'. His penis won't respond to commands like that. An erection is an involuntary reflex that can't be made to happen, it has to be allowed to happen. There are many other parts of the body like that — the heart, lungs, intestines and eyes, etc. — but none seems to cause quite as much worry as the penis.

This natural anxiety is made worse by the fact that it is not something that can be discussed easily. A man usually keeps to himself concerns about the shape, size, appearance and functioning of his penis. He is reluctant to speak to his partner about it, in case she thinks he is odd. He would never dare to ask a male friend in case he were laughed out of the room, and often he feels a doctor would consider his question silly. As we said in our Introduction, the reason we have written this book is to answer questions about sex that men and women are unable to ask anyone around them, but are prepared to ask anonymously on radio.

Apart from worries about size, spots and general appearance of the penis, we got many questions about impotence, partial erections and premature ejaculation. We discuss all these subjects in answer to the following queries.

Question

My penis is about four inches [ten centimetres] long when erect. Is it too small?

Answer

Any penis is quite small when it is not erect and, as many men have probably noticed, their penis varies in size in different conditions. If it is warm, the penis will tend to be longer and when it is cold, the penis will tend to shrivel up. Although the size will vary tremendously when it is not erect, most penises are a similar size when they are erect. Perhaps this is what causes so much concern. Men usually have the opportunity to compare penis size only when they are in the shower or lavatory, not when they are in the bedroom.

You say yours is four inches or thereabouts when erect. If only you understood as much about your sexuality as you do about your tape measure! What you must understand is that penis size has nothing at all to do with satisfying a woman.

Belief that the whole of the vagina plays a major role in arousal and bringing a woman to orgasm is a popular misconception. The vagina is fairly insensitive, except for the lower third. Neither does penis size have anything to do with sexual ability, with being a great lover. It does not reflect masculinity, or sexual interest, or whether women will be attracted to you. Variation in penis size is similar to the fact that some people are thicker set in the body, or taller, or have long or short legs. These are all merely anatomical differences that play no part in a person's character, attractiveness or sexual ability.

There is more to a man than his penis, and if a woman can't look past penis size, or the man gets hooked on believing that by changing his penis, he will change himself, then both are missing out. If you have been in a situation where a woman has laughed at, or commented negatively about, your penis size then I suggest you recognise that for what it is — her problem, not yours. A woman who bases a relationship on the size of a man's penis has got real problems.

Rather than worrying about what she has said, it would be better for you to say something like this to her:

'I am not staying in a relationship where the size of my penis is such an important issue.'

or

'I feel distressed and angry that you would comment on the size of my penis. Are you unhappy with our sexual relationship?'

In the second example, you at least give your partner a chance to discuss what she has said.

However, some men are their own worst enemies. They talk themselves into believing they have a small penis and that, therefore, no woman would ever be attracted to them. As a result, they never really attempt to get into a sexual relationship. If this is happening to you then try telling yourself this:

'I feel anxious about my penis, but I can't change it. But I can change my shyness with women, or my lack of knowledge about sexuality.'

The important thing is not to get a complex about the size of your penis. Instead, concentrate on developing your social skills, and getting to know some women you feel confident with.

Join a club or group where you can do something you enjoy, but at the same time meet new women. It is important to simply make friends in the beginning; don't try to rush headlong into a long-term relationship.

At the same time, start finding out more about sexual relationships. You could read books on the subject (see Recommended Reading), and you could also practise imagining yourself asking a woman what she likes, what turns her on. Women, generally, are pleased to have such a thoughtful and understanding partner, one who asks them what they like, instead of one who assumes he knows what will please her — such as a large penis!

My penis bends down and to the left. Will I be able to have sex?

Answer

A slightly bent penis will not stop you having successful intercourse. It is quite common for a man's penis to bend either one way or the other. This happens because the spaces that fill with blood when the penis is erect are slightly imbalanced so the erect penis has a curve in it.

However, there is a medical problem which produces

a chronic bend in the erect penis that gets progressively worse. It would, therefore, be a good idea to see a urologist, the specialist that deals with this part of the body. Your doctor will give you the referral. Chances are the bend is not a problem, but it is wise to make sure.

Even if the urologist reassures you that all is well, you may still worry that your partner will find your slight curve odd. She may not even notice it, or she may comment on it.

The best plan is to be prepared to deal with whatever may happen. You could say something like this:

'I wondered if you would notice. I feel rather embarrassed about the shape, but there isn't anything wrong. I've seen a doctor about it.'

Then you could explain that it's quite common and give the reason for it, as we have above. And remember, even though something like a bent penis seems really obvious to the person who has it, often other people don't notice it. So don't overplay it in your head. Keep it in perspective. If it doesn't interfere with intercourse or enjoying the sexual relationship, then it is not a problem. It will only become one if you allow yourself to worry about it too much.

In answer to the previous question we advised the listener not to get a complex about his penis. We advised him, instead, to concentrate on developing social skills. The same applies to you.

Question

I have spots on my penis. Is this the sign of a disease?

Answer

More than likely, spots on your penis indicate a localised skin infection, such as pimples or acne. However, one cannot rule out the risk of your having a sexually transmitted disease, particularly if you have had casual sex, or if your partner has had sex with someone else.

Don't leave it to chance. Go and see your doctor. If you would rather not discuss this with your usual doctor, then go to the nearest sexually transmitted disease clinic. We have listed the major clinics in capital cities, under Support Organisations. Whether you go to your own doctor, or an STD clinic, you may feel a little embarrassed about it. Quite frankly, some doctors don't handle such problems particularly well. On the other hand, there are many doctors who are used to people being apprehensive about this situation, and who will be very helpful. So if you don't feel comfortable with one doctor, remember you have every right to make an appointment with someone else.

A tip about overcoming your reluctance to make an appointment — try saying this to yourself a few times:

'I know I will feel embarrassed going to the doctor with this particular problem, but it is important for my future health that I get it cleared up. I will simply make myself go.'

If you are young and need to tell your parents before you visit the doctor, then plan to make a simple, straightforward statement such as:

'Mum (or Dad) I am worried about spots around my genital area. I would like to make an appointment with the doctor.'

It may be a little embarrassing, but it is much better to find out than to risk serious health problems, or to feel worried all the time.

You may find it easier to go to a sexually transmitted disease clinic because its staff is specially trained to discuss such things. If you *have* contracted a sexually transmitted disease, and you are in a long-term relationship, you must let your partner know. Your local STD clinic will advise you about how to break the news to your partner. Before starting any new sexual relationships you must be frank about disease (see Chapter 1).

Question

I saw my local GP because of a swelling in my penis and testes. He tested me for gonorrhoea. The tests were negative. Now the swelling has come back, and it is accompanied by acute pain.

Answer

Go straight to your local communicable diseases clinic, or back to your GP. It is essential you act immediately, and persevere until you discover what is wrong. Pain and swelling do not happen if everything is in good, healthy working order. (See also the answer to the previous question.)

Question

When I get an erection, my foreskin does not stretch back and the head of my penis can't get out. Consequently, the erection is bent. It is affecting my sex life with my wife to a marked degree. What can I do about it?

Answer

It is called Peyroni's disease. It is the invasion of not only the penis, but also hands and feet, by a fibrous tissue which, as time progresses, contracts. It is possible to operate on Peyroni's disease. You would have to see a urologist or a plastic surgeon. Get your local doctor to give you a referral.

Question

One of my testicles hangs lower than the other one. I am 17, and I have only noticed it in the past couple of years. It hangs about five or six centimetres further down than the other one, which is quite normal to look at. Will it affect my fertility later on in life?

Answer

Probably not. It does not sound like a serious problem, but it would be best to see a doctor to make certain.

Question

I am only 13 and I have a pimple on the tip of my penis. It is yellow and looks as if there is pus inside it. I have no reason to believe it is sexually transmitted because I haven't had any sex yet. I'm too embarrassed to go to my parents. What can I do?

Answer

The young caller was not too keen on going to the family doctor either! However, he did have a good relationship going with his sister, who was quite a few years older than him, so he agreed that he would go to her in order to get some medical help.

Question

My penis does not erect vertically. I can have an erection quite easily, however, it moves to my left side by about four centimetres. There is no pain if I push it and hold it straight, which I can do without any effort.

**Could this have been caused by my method of mas-
turbation, which was to lie face-down on my bed and
move about? Will the bend affect my married life in
the future? Please help as it concerns me greatly.
Don't tell me to go to a doctor as I am only 13.**

Answer

It sounds perfectly normal, with no dire consequences
for your future sex life or fertility. It most probably would
not have been caused by anything other than your genes.
Unless it gets painful, develops lesions or a discharge, it
is highly unlikely you will have to visit a doctor.

Question

**My penis is very large and my partner complains. We
both want to have sex, but it is physically impossible
because my penis is just too big for her vagina. What
can we do?**

Answer

The real problem here is probably that you have a poor
sexual relationship, not that you have a large penis.

Your partner is more likely to be complaining because
she is not sufficiently aroused, therefore she is not sufficiently lubricated, and her pain is due to having intercourse when her vagina is not ready. You probably have
the attitude that because your penis is larger than other
men's, that is enough to turn her on, and you have left
your knowledge of sex right there. You have not learnt
how to arouse your partner.

There is no such thing as a penis that is too large. A
woman's vagina is very flexible and can accommodate
any sized penis. The vagina is flat — not tube-like — but

during sexual arousal, it lubricates and lengthens and balloons out, making it flexible enough for a penis of any size.

A woman may find some intercourse positions uncomfortable when her partner's penis touches her cervix. If this is the case, then all you have to do is change positions. Try different ones until you discover the one that is most comfortable.

Another important point to mention here is that a woman needs to learn how to arouse herself so that she can tell her partner what she likes him to do for her (see Chapter 3). A man needs to listen to what she wants. If the above information does not seem to solve the problem, then you should see a qualified psychologist to help you sort things out.

Question

I can't get an erection. What can I do?

Answer

This is a very frustrating problem. It is also extremely common. Most men, at some time in their lives, would have had difficulty getting an erection.

It happens for all sorts of reasons and sometimes these are totally unrelated to the sexual relationship. You only have to be tired, worried about work, or upset about something that has happened in the family, and you can find yourself having trouble getting an erection. At times like these you would be better not to attempt sex at all. Sit and cuddle your partner, or go for a walk, or do something relaxing that you both enjoy doing together.

Most men refuse to believe that the problem can be psychological. They are much more comfortable with the belief that it is a purely physical problem, and really have trouble coming to terms with the fact that it might be all 'in their heads'. The majority of erection problems *are* psychological and not physical.

However, it is important to make sure you don't fall into that minority who do have a physical problem. The first step in working this out is to decide whether or not you have trouble getting erections in all circumstances. For example, can you get an erection when you masturbate, or can you get an erection with one partner and not another?

If you answered yes to either of these questions, then you probably need to look for psychological reasons.

If your answer was no, you must go to a urologist. Your doctor will give you a referral.

If you answered yes, but are still not convinced that the problem is in your head, you should also pay your doctor a visit. Once you have ruled out any possibility that the problem is physical, you need to work out why you are stuck with it.

If the problem is psychological, probably it sprang from simple beginnings, but because you worried about it so much you compounded the problem. For example, did you begin to have problems with your erection after not being able to have intercourse one night when you were tired, or had had too much to drink? If so, the next time you went to have intercourse you probably found yourself wondering whether you would be able to get an erection this time. You may have asked yourself, 'What if I can't?'.

If this picture fits you, then no matter how it all started, what is keeping it going is *you*. Your worry stops you relaxing and enjoying sex, and that in turn stops you having an erection. You need to take some simple steps to overcome that worry. Try the following exercise.

Imagine yourself having an enjoyable sexual time with your wife or girlfriend, without having an erection. Imagine every possible thing you could do to turn her on and at the same time enjoy yourself, but still not have an erection. Go over this again and again, in your mind. Your imagination plays an important part in your enjoyment of sex.

If you find it impossible to imagine yourself enjoying sex without an erection then you need to do some more sexual homework. Try to get hold of videos or books that the two of you find erotic.

Start exploring what you can do that is enjoyable without having an erection or intercourse. At this stage it is very important that you don't even attempt to have intercourse.

If you and your partner find you can't come to terms with this exercise, then you may have an attitude towards sex that you need to change. Often the belief that you can't enjoy yourself or satisfy your partner, without having an erection and intercourse, puts pressure on you, the man. That belief, or pressure, is what makes lack of an erection a certainty for most men at some time in their lives.

If you *have* been able to imagine yourself enjoying sex without an erection, then your next step is to do just that. Speak to your partner, and if she is happy with the arrangement, practise making love without intercourse. In other words, put into practice what you have until now been imagining. Try to practise feeling comfortable without an erection during lovemaking. At this time learn to say to yourself:

'I feel somewhat strange if I lose my erection during loveplay, but I know there are lots of other things I can do, particularly to my partner, that are enjoyable. If I don't worry I will eventually get my erection back.'

When you honestly feel comfortable about not having an erection or intercourse during loveplay, it is time to start including it.

To follow the above suggestions successfully you

need a co-operative partner. If you have no partner at the moment you can still practise the parts that involve your imagination. Should your partner not be co-operative, then you probably have a more complicated relationship problem, and we recommend you seek further help. You will also need to seek help if you still can't get an erection despite all your hard work with the above suggestions.

Question

I have read that there is a drug which, injected into the penis, keeps it erect for hours. What is it and where do I go to get it? I can't keep erect long enough for my wife, despite visits to a psychologist and medical tests that show there is nothing physically wrong with me.

Answer

There are some urologists in Australia using the drug, and that is where you would have to go for the treatment. Obviously, you have already seen a urologist if you have been physically checked for abnormal blood-flow to the penis, etc.

Only resort to this drug under strict psychological and medical supervision. It is called papavarine and is administered in amounts measured to correspond with the length of time you want to remain erect.

For some men, whose erection problems are psychological, it can have spectacular effects. Being able to have an erect penis this way can make them feel so good about themselves that it obliterates whatever doubts they had. Just as spectacular can be its effect on some physically impaired men. The emphasis is on the word *some* in both cases. If not administered in a responsible and caring manner, the reverse can as easily apply and the patient can become dependent on papavarine injections for intercourse.

Question

I can only get a partial erection. Why is this?

Answer

A partial erection or the inability to ejaculate often means you are anxious about something. It happens particularly in new sexual relationships. Understandably, you can be a bit up-tight with a new sexual partner and therefore sexual responses slow down.

One of the best ways to relax in this situation is to let your partner know how you feel. You could simply say to her:

'I feel anxious about beginning a new sexual relationship. I would like it to work well, but at the moment I am having trouble ejaculating.'

Then do something together that is pleasant and affectionate, but not directly related to sex. If it is an on-going problem and not related to a new sexual encounter, you will need to go to a urologist. Your doctor will give you a referral. If there is nothing wrong physically, see a psychologist.

Question

I suffer from premature ejaculation. Would a lotion help?

Answer

There are all sorts of lotions, potions and gadgets on offer that claim to solve this problem for men. However, they are based on the wrong assumptions about premature ejaculation.

Some men think their partners are not having orgasms solely because they are not lasting long enough in intercourse. And 'hey presto!', they brand themselves premature ejaculators.

Real premature ejaculation is when a man comes before intercourse or within seconds of it beginning. And we mean seconds: two or three.

The majority of so-called premature ejaculators do not fit into this category. So it is a fair statement to say that most men who think they suffer from premature ejaculation, or come too quickly, simply do not!

A man will usually come to this conclusion all on his own, without ever consulting the woman. Sometimes it is simply based on a general comment by the woman that she is not enjoying sex, which is not pursued any further, or the man imagines she is thinking this.

Unfortunately, men still believe that they are responsible for their own arousal and the arousal of their partners, and that the only way to do this is to make intercourse last longer. No one can take responsibility for another's arousal. If your partner is not becoming aroused then you should both read Chapter 3.

Men often fear they are not satisfying their partners, but they never actually ask them how they feel. If your partner is not being responsive, you should ask her what the problem is. You could try saying:

'When we have sex you lie still. Is there something wrong?'

The pause and squeeze techniques have been used to help solve the problem of premature ejaculation. However, they were developed about twenty years ago, and were based on the incorrect assumption that lengthening the time of intercourse would improve the sexual relationship. The woman, once again, was not asked what she liked.

If you *do* find yourself ejaculating more quickly than you wish to, a very simple way to solve the problem is to have sex more frequently, or to masturbate more often. (By depleting your reserves of semen, you'll reduce the likelihood of premature ejaculation.)

In some cases, ejaculating too quickly is associated with high levels of tension and anxiety. Often the man has a chronic case of anxiety and, when he has sex, the high tension leads to quick ejaculation, usually without much orgasmic satisfaction. His anxiety may be due to a tendency to worry about most things, or it may be due to stress. It may also be specifically associated with sex and relationships with women.

It is beyond the scope of this book to deal in detail with these problems, so our standard advice also applies here: go and see a psychologist who has the training and experience to help you sort out your individual reason for reacting in this way.

Listeners Share Experiences

You will find this hard to believe, but it is true. I am really depressed about having a large penis. I've discovered that girls I've had relationships with have talked about it, and now I know that the last two only went out with me to have a look at it. I knew them pretty well, getting to know them before we had sex. But I obviously didn't get to know them well enough.

My foreskin underneath my penis catches. I don't think I was circumcised properly. It hasn't worried me until now. I'm 17 and becoming more sexually active, and get embarrassed at how my erection looks.

Chapter Six

What Do You Want from Sex?

If your answer is 'erotic pleasure, and heaps of it', then good for you, because basically you are on the right track. The only real desire that is satisfied by sex is the desire for erotic pleasure.

However, no one will always have sex for the sake of erotic pleasure alone. We satisfy many other needs when we have sex with a lover. Through sex we gain: closeness and intimacy; relaxation; the chance to be alone with the one we love; the fun and enjoyment of sharing something together; attention from our partner; and, of course, the giving and receiving of pleasure and the expression of our sexual feelings in arousal and orgasm.

Providing you are both on the same track, that is, both after erotic pleasure, then sex will be good. Add any of the above to that and you will still be okay. But if only one of you is after erotic pleasure and the other is using sex exclusively for any of the above reasons, then expect the relationship to run into problems.

The most common expression of a problem generated this way is the complaint that one person in a relationship wants more sex than the other. On radio, such a statement was often quickly followed by a tense question, 'Is there something wrong with me? Am I over-sexed?'.

You don't have to be a genius to see that it is only a matter of time before this problem extends itself into the rest of the relationship, if it is allowed to go unchecked. So it is essential to know what you want from sex, and essential to be honest about it.

Sit down and examine what you really want when you have sex, particularly if you are unhappy with the frequency of sex. Take those other needs we have mentioned, one at a time, and ask yourself:

'When I have sex do I want:
- attention from my partner?
- time alone?
- affection?
- to share some special fun and enjoyment?
- a feeling of closeness and intimacy?
- sensual pleasure?
    or
- the erotic pleasure of sex?'

If you find that you (or your partner) often have sex when you are really seeking fulfilment of the first six needs listed above, you may like to consider the following alternative ways of meeting these needs.

ATTENTION

- Sit together and talk about your day, without interruptions.
- Hold hands and go for a walk.
- Sit down and, looking at each other, discuss your future, your interests, your dreams, something either of you would like to achieve.
- Interrupt whatever you are doing occasionally to ring or visit your partner.

- Speak exclusively to your partner for a few minutes when you are in a large group of people.

TIME ALONE

- Develop an interest the two of you can enjoy doing together, exclusively.
- Make sure you have dinner together at home a couple of times a week, with no children and absolutely no interruptions.
- Go OUT to dinner together regularly.
- Play a sport both of you enjoy.

AFFECTION

- There are thousands of ways to express this without it leading to sex — hugging, kissing, holding hands, standing with your arms around each other.
- Discuss and then agree to an arrangement where both of you can freely express your affection in ways that don't embarrass or worry the giver or the receiver, and satisfy both.
- Another good thing to do is to give surprise gifts — small signs of having thought of the other person.
- Write affectionate notes.

FUN AND ENJOYMENT

- Discover together what gives you both a sense of fun — what makes you laugh and perhaps even feel like children.
- Learn to really 'let your hair down' together.

CLOSENESS AND INTIMACY

- Communicate important feelings, including the bad ones.
- Compliment the other person on something that he or she has done well, or on how he or she looks.
- Share an intimate dinner, discussing important positive feelings.
- Go over past good and bad times that are now part of the good memories that you have between you.
- Lie in bed hugging and talking about plans for the day or something you are going to do in the future.

SENSUAL PLEASURE

- Try all-over body touching and stroking or massage that doesn't lead to touching the genitals, having an orgasm or intercourse.
- If either of you becomes aroused, ask the other person whether he or she would like to have sex, but if the answer is no, stop at the massage. (This may be somewhat frustrating for the partner who is more interested in moving on to sex, but persevere because you will find that in the long run sex will be more enjoyable.)

So these are suggestions for alternative activities you can share together if you are falling into the trap of having sex when it is really something else you desire. If you and your partner learn to express your loving feelings in the ways outlined above, your sexual relationship will almost certainly benefit in the process.

Now we will discuss the last, most direct reason, for wanting to have sex.

EROTIC PLEASURE

For maximum erotic pleasure, only have sex when both of you really want to. Given these circumstances, obviously the erotic pleasure of your sexual relationship will increase. However, this will happen only if you are prepared to be honest and say no when you are NOT interested.

When you *do* say no, ask your partner what would come close to satisfying him or her. It could be affection, time together or any of the activities suggested above. If your partner can come up with something else, then do that instead. Sometimes this concept is hard for couples to grasp, and that is understandable. But it really works: if you don't feel like sex and suggest something else you'll feel more relaxed and eventually, when you do have sex with your partner, you'll be really interested.

For the person wanting sex, accepting your partner's refusal, coping with your frustration and then willingly doing something else, will do much more for your sexual relationship than if you sulk or attempt to manipulate your partner into agreeing to sex he or she doesn't want.

It is important to spend some time here discussing the consequences of just 'going along' with what a partner wants. Many sexual relationships seem to go downhill when one person does this solely to please a partner. Deep down, that person will feel resentful and unhappy. The other partner picks up these feelings of resentment and, in an attempt to feel wanted again, tries to have sex more frequently. Consciously, or subconsciously, he or she believes it will solve the problems. Sadly, it just makes things much worse. No matter how unintentionally, 'going along' affects your feelings towards your partner. It can open a Pandora's Box of problems for the relationship.

PUTTING THEORIES INTO PRACTICE

Of course, it's much easier to read about ways to solve problems than to actually put them into practice. Obviously, no one can change overnight. This doesn't matter. In fact, gradual changes are more likely to become permanent than overnight conversions.

The following steps may help you to improve your sexual relationship.

- Ask yourself why you do/don't want to have sex with your partner. This should help you to understand your present reactions.
- Now work out how you could change your reactions to improve the relationship.
- Don't expect your new reactions to be perfect every time. At first concentrate on changing the reaction you feel is wrong about every third time. Then aim for every second time, and then nearly every time, etc.
- Set yourself some simple guidelines, and don't move on to the next step until you are reasonably consistent in the one you are working on.

The two following examples show how these ideas can be put into practice.

HER PROBLEM

Cheryl identified her needs as time alone with her husband and erotic pleasure from sex. When she thought about her sexual relationship she realised that she had never really initiated either sex or time alone for other activities. She used to get annoyed when her husband went off and did things by himself, nagging that they didn't spend enough time together. She had felt happy with their lovemaking at first, but had recently felt increasingly left out, as though she was not getting anything for herself out of sex.

Cheryl had taken the first steps towards change. She could see what she was doing wrong, and she knew the changes she wanted to make. Now she just had to work out how to incorporate them into her behaviour.

. . . AND SOLUTION

After discussing it with her husband, Cheryl decided to think of things she would like them to do together, places they would enjoy going to. As well, they agreed that she would initiate sex at least once a week.

Then gradually, she would work up to organising an outing with her husband every week, and initiating sex just when she felt like it. She would also begin to ask for things she liked in the sexual relationship.

Cheryl took into account the fact that she must expect to feel silly at times, planning her behaviour in this detailed way. She took comfort in knowing her husband was with her all the way and that when she got over this awkwardness, things would become more spontaneous. Most of all, she would be getting something for herself out of sex and getting more enjoyment from her relationship with her husband.

HIS PROBLEM

Geoff had felt frustrated and annoyed that he was constantly being refused when he initiated sex with his wife.

They had been married ten years, and for about the past six years his wife had become less and less interested in sex.

When he sat down and assessed the relationship he realised that he was only close to her when they had sex. He had never shown interest in her activities, he never held her hand or kissed her, and he rarely paid much attention to her. He also worked out, with her help, that showing affection had always been a problem for him. To alter such long-standing patterns, they knew they would both have to work on the change.

. . . AND SOLUTION

Geoff decided to start things rolling by making himself express his good feelings towards his wife in ways other than sexually. He set the small goal of practising doing this just once a day. It would be either a kiss, a hug or a smile whenever he felt good.

Once he'd achieved this, he increased these demonstrations of affection to twice a day, and after that they gradually became more frequent until they occurred relatively spontaneously.

As well, he began to invite affection from his wife, so that instead of initiating sex when he simply wanted to be close, he would ask for affection.

IN SUMMARY

Whether men are having trouble expressing their feelings or women are finding it difficult to be overtly sexual, either sex can change. It just takes perception, planning and patient persistence. If you can't organise this for yourself, find a good psychologist to guide you.

Question

I think our sexual relationship has become monumentally boring. My wife doesn't seem to be interested any more. What should we do?

Answer

Many of the sexual 'how to' manuals imply that the way around this is to 'try something new' or 'become more sensual' or 'have sex on the fridge'. Frankly, if you are bored with your sexual relationship, none of these things will work. As for sex on the fridge, it can be downright life-threatening!

Occasionally couples may, for a while, find it interesting to try something new, but this is not getting to the core of the problem. Lack of intimacy, or time shared together, is more often the cause of boredom. New places, positions or partners, for that matter, will not solve the problem.

You need to take stock of your relationship. The fact that you say 'My wife doesn't seem to be . . .' implies that you have not asked her, and don't know what she is really thinking or feeling. You may both need to improve your general communication or, if you feel this is good, then look at the communication in your sexual relationship.

You may both find it difficult and embarrassing talking about your sexual feelings and thoughts, but overcoming this embarrassment and sharing more about yourself with your partner is very important. It is normal to feel hesitant at first in discussions like this. Be prepared to keep going, to push yourself, and you will discover that gradually you become more comfortable opening up to each other in this way.

Be prepared to hear things that you may find upsetting or even hurtful. Similarly, you will have things to say to your wife that may be hard for her to accept. It is essential that you are honest about your thoughts and feelings, even if it upsets you both at first. The consolation is that once you have got past this point, you may then be able to solve some of the things that are not quite right. And you will be well on your way to a much better sexual relationship.

If the two of you can't work this out alone, go to a properly qualified psychologist.

Question

My partner and I have been trying to find her G-spot. Where is it? And is it as good as it sounds?

Answer

Probably not! We can hear all those who swear by it protesting as we write, as indeed they often protested on radio about our attitude to the G-spot. As with any new discovery, the accompanying hype gives the impression that it is larger than life. The reality can be quite different. By the same token, we hasten to say that for couples who have found a G-spot and are experiencing the pleasures of their discovery, then that is terrific. Enjoy it!

But for those who have not yet hit the spot (if it exists) then there is nothing you can gain by worrying about what you *might* be missing out on. By all means explore and try to find it in a fun way together. But never let yourself become anxious because you can't find the latest fashionable sexual position.

The search could catapult you into a situation where sex becomes like a race or competition, the winner being the person who can achieve orgasm the greatest number of times, have five erections in one night or find the elusive G-spot.

People should enjoy sex their own way, with their own set of self-discovered sexual turn-ons. And it doesn't have to include anything that you have heard or read that other people enjoy. Sex is not a 'keeping up with the Joneses' activity.

The enjoyment in a sexual relationship is less tangible than using certain positions to reach orgasm. Good sex is a combination of physical and emotional arousal: the physical achieved by using techniques that are a turn-on for both partners; the emotional, by sharing sexual feelings and thoughts. The type of sexual techniques you use will not make a lot of difference to the *enjoyment* in your relationship.

Having beaten you about the ears a bit first, let us now answer your question! The G-spot was named after the German, Grafenberg, who first documented it. He found that some women, particularly those who reached orgasm during intercourse, reported they got stimulation from a specific area just inside the vagina, under the pubic bone. The size of this area varies from that of a two dollar coin to a twenty cent coin. The position reportedly is on the back of the front wall of the vagina, a little to one side.

It is probably easier for the woman to find out if she has a sensitive spot here with the help of her partner, and initially fingers will be more practical than his penis. With the woman lying on her back, he inserts two fingers (fingertips facing up) into the lower third of her vagina, and gently explores that wall at the back of the pubic hair.

Some women have told us on radio that it is a similar feeling to having their clitoris stimulated. For each of those women, though, there are thousands who feel nothing at all. So don't expect too much, but you never know. You may be onto your sexual discovery of a lifetime!

The fascination with the G-spot reminds us of the

reaction on our radio program when a super new sexual technique was mentioned on the popular television series, *LA Law*. One of the characters performed what he called a Venus Butterfly on his sexual partner, with obviously devastatingly delightful effect — but no 'how to' details. Listeners could not get to the phone quickly enough to ask us what it was.

We rang the creators of this series, the American CBS network. A spokesperson, when asked the much-touted question, 'What is a Venus Butterfly?', replied, 'I have no idea! Your guess is as good as mine. It was invented by the writers of the show to get them out of a storyline. They had a bigamist with twelve very devoted, beautiful wives, and no one could explain the secret of his success. So they invented the Venus Butterfly.'

We are sure some people were disappointed with this answer, but most accepted it with good humour. The enormous response to this episode of *LA Law* is a sad reflection of people's desire to find a mythical key to the perfect sexual relationship.

Question

My girlfriend never wants the same thing twice when we have sex. Sometimes I don't know whether she has come. It is a bit confusing.

Answer

Talk her into giving you some sign that she has had an orgasm. It doesn't have to be verbal. As for keeping you on your toes with what kind of stimulation she requires, it is probably because she is well tuned into her needs. However, she shouldn't keep you in the dark about this. You could tell her you are uncertain but want to co-operate, and ask her to explain more clearly before you make love what she wants. This can be done in a playful way during foreplay. It doesn't have to be reeled off like a shopping list. What she wanted last week or last night need not be what she will want tonight. Don't let it frighten you, because it is a good sign.

Question

Some mornings I wake up and feel really ashamed at what I allowed myself to do with my boyfriend during sex the night before. He asks me to dress up and act out scenes and become people we know. Other times he wants me to take the dominant role, being a male.

But what seems to upset me the most is when he wants me to be a schoolgirl. I suppose the last one upsets me so much because I started having sex when I was 12. I had no idea what I was doing then. I'm 35 now and I experience a horrible conflict when I do that for him.

Sometimes I find it all exciting, but only sometimes. He is always interested in sex like this, so I forget my feelings and get carried away in giving him pleasure, but the next morning I feel really bad. What should I do?

Answer

This reflects what a lot of people feel about certain things in their sexual relationships: that they like SOME things SOME of the time.

Boredom will soon set in if you cave in to demands you feel uncomfortable with — not to mention what will happen to your self-respect. Listen to what you want deep down, and act on that. There seems to be a lack of tenderness and intimacy in your relationship, so explore these areas together.

Question

If I pressure my wife into sex it is likely she will say, 'Oh, go ahead and get it over with', but I don't want it to be like that. I am not really game enough to try pressuring her, anyway, because suffering her aggression and lack of interest is too unpleasant. Normally she is a very gentle lady who is embarrassed by sex. We have been together twelve years. I'm 63 and she is 55. I have put up with this for the past nine years. It seems that she has no interest whatsoever in sex. But I DO, and I want to have more sex. Is my sex life to end here at 63? I enjoy sex and I am quite capable of it. However, I do not want to leave my wife. I respect the woman and love her very much. Please don't tell me to talk to her. I would have to be as game as Ned Kelly to do that.

Answer

Anyone in your situation — and there are many — has the fear that a relationship will be rocked or shattered by unravelling what has gone wrong. The temptation to leave things as they are can be overwhelming. While it will be a gamble — no one can be sure which way it will go — you might as well try to make things better, because at the moment *you* are losing. You have to talk to her. Say exactly what you have said here. Then persevere, no matter how unpleasant or uncomfortable the initial outcome.

Open with something like, 'I feel really unhappy about our sexual relationship. I have tried to deal with the problem for the past nine years, and I can't. I am thinking of seeing someone about it, and would like you to come along, too. Our relationship is very good for me, except for sex, and I don't want to jeopardise it. Try to tell me how you feel about this.'

You might have to preface this with a silent 'One, two, three, go!' — and launch straight into it. Give her as much information as you can, and ask her to do the same for you. But be straightforward, because you can't afford to be subtle about things now. State your case honestly and openly.

As for Ned Kelly — sometimes it is comparatively easy to do things that are physically courageous. Saying something really important about an issue that means a lot to you can be much, much harder. You will end up gamer than Ned. If she says no, then it is up to you, but you may have to leave the relationship.

Question

Do men want the same from a sexual relationship as women?

Answer

The answer to this simple question is very complex. It depends on who is around at the time you ask a man what he wants from sex.

If he is in a large group he will tend to fall back on stereotypical answers: heavy emphasis on physical attributes of a partner, importance of sex, frequency, etc., but with very little emphasis on feelings or intimacy. Ask when he is alone and the answer is very different.

The latter was particularly evident on radio where a man was in a one-to-one situation, with the added bonus of being anonymous. In this situation, the feelings and concerns expressed by men were similar to those of female callers.

Men *do* worry about what a partner is thinking, how she feels about their sexual relationship. They *do* like sharing intimacy, they *do* need cuddling and reassurance and they *don't* always want to have sex. Unfortunately, some men still have difficulty admitting this, and particular difficulty expressing it.

This is not surprising if theirs was an upbringing that emphasised strength, control and power. Any feelings or sensitivity would long ago have been submerged, lost early in childhood, when they learnt to deny things that might make them look as if they were not strong and in control.

Men conditioned in this way often find that the only acceptable way to express close feelings for another person is to have sex with them. This is often the cause of the common problem of a man wanting sex more frequently than his partner does. Sex is his only legitimate expression of intimacy.

The reverse of this problem for men is women who have trouble owning up to feeling sexual desire, let alone giving full rein to its expression in a relationship.

In a large group, women usually respond with vague, romantic ideals when asked about sexual relationships. They will never be explicit about sex. Yet, get a woman on her own and you will find that she *does* want the erotic pleasure of a sexual relationship, she *does* want to be overtly sexual with a partner, she *does* want to be aroused and reach orgasm.

Women are NOT just interested in being romantically wooed without any follow up. But because it was not considered 'nice' or 'ladylike' for girls to have sexual feelings, many women have learnt to ignore their erotic sexual desire and substitute intimacy, affection, or anything other than what would really satisfy them.

These statements are obviously generalisations, but after talking with hundreds of listeners over a period of five years, these are the impressions we have gained.

We have a long way to go if the similarities between the sexes are to be recognised and encouraged. Education from a very early age is necessary for men and women to really learn to express the wide range of emotions they possess. This would result in some women being more dominant and controlling, and some men being softer and more sensitive. It is an ideal that perhaps all of us can try to address for the future, through our children.

More practically, how does one deal with these differences in an individual relationship? Begin by just discussing together how you were brought up to think about sexual relationships, trying to gain some understanding of your past influences. This understanding will not be enough to change how you are now, but it can be important to recognise that some of your attitudes are based on things you learnt at an impressionable age, when you had no control over what you were being taught.

The good news is that, as an adult, you are responsible for yourself. Blaming the past will not change you. But recognising what happened will help you to take that responsibility for your present attitudes.

Chapter Seven

ORAL SEX

Oral sex seems to cause a lot of controversy. On radio, this subject could always be relied on to get people involved. The discussions would be a vigorous mix of complaint that 'such a thing' was being talked about, praise of the 'if only it had been discussed in my day' type and information-seeking. Reactions could be extreme. In the early days of the program Helen received a death threat for talking about oral sex.

Perhaps the severity of this reaction and the general shock and negativity towards the subject reflects the discomfort a lot of people still feel about anything to do with the genitals.

Some people also think of the genitals as 'dirty' because of their proximity to the anus and the urethra. The penis in particular suffers from this association, which, of course, is wrong. Any part of the body that is not washed gets dirty. Genitals are neither more nor less dirty than hands, ears or teeth, and need the same attention to cleaning.

However, at the outset it should be clearly stated that many of the common sexually transmitted diseases can be spread in the throat. Consequently, before having oral sex with a new partner you both need to discuss frankly any possibility that either of you may have come in contact with such diseases (see Chapter 1).

Another speculation about our discomfort in discussing oral sex is that it could be tied to our protestant work ethic background — the one that does not really permit behaviour purely for pleasure. Masturbation suffered in the same way, although the more widely recognised it becomes as necessary to our sexual development, the easier we become.

While people may feel uncomfortable talking about oral sex, it's fair to say the majority participate in it. Consider this: in America in the 1950s, Kinsey's study showed that 50 per cent of people had engaged in oral sex at a time when, in some American states, it was an illegal sexual activity. On radio reaction alone, thirty years on and in a country where it is not illegal, we are very interested indeed in oral sex.

It's worth mentioning another reason why oral sex has been considered unacceptable behaviour: in the past it was assumed that this was the way homosexual people made love. Given the narrow, bigoted attitude of a huge proportion of Australians to homosexuality in the past, it's easy to see how most considered oral sex was not something a 'nice' heterosexual couple did. It was thought of as immature and most certainly not 'proper' behaviour. But it is not a sign of being afflicted with some weird psychological problem. Oral sex is a legitimate expression of sexual desire, practised by a large number of couples.

As we have already discussed in Chapter 3, many women find it easier to achieve orgasm with oral sex or manual stimulation of the clitoris than during intercourse. This is a facetious thought, but this may be just the justification we have been waiting for to make oral sex more acceptable: that some women need to be orally stimulated to reach orgasm. And as everyone knows we all have a right to have an orgasm! (We are joking because it is not necessary to justify any type of sexual behaviour as long as it doesn't harm your partner and is not illegal.)

A telling point about the acceptability or non-acceptability of human behaviour is how it is portrayed in film or literature. We rarely see lovers in films or on our television screens participating in oral sex. While it may be more commonly mentioned in literature, in both films and books it's more often than not relegated to the area of pornography.

Despite all this, as we have mentioned, it seems many people do use oral sex as part of their lovemaking, and they derive a great deal of pleasure from it. There are others who would like to try oral sex, but are held back by uncertainty. And there are other couples where one partner wants it, but the other refuses. All these problems will be discussed in the following questions and answers.

Hygiene is one of the first things people ask about when they have managed to bring up the subject. A lot of people are surprised to know that the mouth carries more germs than the genitals, a point which is worth making to keep the cleanliness–genitals issue in perspective. But, of course, general cleanliness is important, more for aesthetics than anything else.

If you find that pubic hair gets in the way, get rid of some of it. Women can safely remove or trim hair from the outer major lips of the vagina, leaving most of the pubic hair in front covering the pubic bone.

Discuss ejaculation. Some people don't like the thought of swallowing semen, so make sure you clear up this point before you start to have sex. If there is any possibility that the male partner has a sexually transmitted disease, the woman certainly shouldn't swallow semen.

Make sure you are assertive enough to let your partner know if you feel uncomfortable in any way when you are making love like this. For example, there are some oral sex positions in which you may feel suffocated. Good communication is especially important here if you want to change things.

Finally, if, after oral sex, you contract a sore throat you will need to check that you have not got a sexually transmitted disease. Go to a general practitioner or to your nearest STD clinic (see Support Organisations).

Question

I would like to try oral sex with my partner, but I'm not sure what his reaction will be when I mention it. How can I ask him?

Answer

Words are not the only form of communication we humans use. We get messages across to each other with a wide range of non-verbal cues. This probably happens more so in a close personal relationship. We do it with eye contact, the tone of our voices, stance, touch, and so on. Obviously, communication is the answer to this problem, but if you feel too awkward to say something try a non-verbal cue. When you are making love, just initiate oral sex. Be as tentative or definite as you feel is appropriate. Your partner will signal that it is all right fairly quickly. If this doesn't work — if, for example, he reacts with surprise or shock — you will then have to be prepared to talk.

Don't just leave it and hope that the next time he might be more relaxed about it. If anything he might be more nervous of having sex with you. So it is very important to talk if this has been his reaction.

A suggested opening is:

'I feel awkward talking about oral sex, but I would like to try it, if that is what you want too.'

Then perhaps you could try reading some accurate information about it together — this chapter, for example — and, when you are both ready, try again. For more information, see Recommended Reading.

Should either one of you have trouble reaching orgasm with oral sex — if it seems to take a long time and you lose interest — then you would be better off switching to some other form of arousal.

Unless you are both happy it's best not to attempt new techniques all the time, otherwise the whole lovemaking situation can get boring and unpleasant. By all means, keep including oral sex in your sexual activity and, as it gets easier, you will find yourself associating it with arousal. It will give pleasure and add another dimension to your lovemaking. But be patient, don't expect too much from it at first.

The reverse may happen, of course. From your very first attempt you could find oral sex extremely arousing, which, of course, you are unlikely to see as a problem.

Question

My partner is against oral sex. What can I do?

Answer

Let's say at the outset that the way this question is posed doesn't put the person asking it in a very flattering light. To say the least, it's selfish, but more about that in a moment.

If only one of you is interested in oral sex, there may be a number of reasons for it. Many who push a partner towards this may be simply seeking more stimulation. They may be with a partner who isn't giving them enough to lead to arousal and orgasm.

Some seize on oral sex because it has a big reputation as a technique, and they feel it has to be the answer for their lack of arousal. It *isn't* necessarily the answer. And that is important to realise here. No particular sexual technique is necessary for an exciting, happy sex life. If one (or both of you) doesn't feel happy with something, then there are other things you can do together. You don't have to include oral sex in your lovemaking.

If one partner is enduring something in the sexual relationship just because the other person wants, or demands, it, then that is a formula for disaster in the long term.

The person doing the demanding is after the enjoyment of oral sex at the cost of the other partner's feelings. You probably don't see yourself in this light, but that is the implication of your question.

It says much more about your relationship as a whole rather than just your sexual relationship: that you wish to get your way and you dismiss your partner's point of view as 'wrong'. It is an approach that often leads to a stand-off situation along the following lines: 'I want you to have oral sex so you should change' versus 'You don't take my feelings into account at all'.

A different approach will often elicit a very different response. Try showing respect for your partner's feelings in your attitude and approach. Say something like:

'I know you feel uncomfortable about this but I wondered if we could try it, and if you still feel unhappy about it in any way, let me know.'

The reaction will usually be one of:

'I do feel uncomfortable about it, but I can tell it really means a lot to you, and you've been so concerned about my point of view that I'd like to give it a try again.'

Being understanding and considerate will win hands-down over a selfish, demanding attitude.

Question

My partner would like to have oral sex, but is uncertain about it. How can I reassure her?

Answer

Discuss together exactly what it is about oral sex that is making your partner uncomfortable.

Is it hygiene? Then this is overcome with washing (as long as neither of you have a sexually transmitted disease). As mentioned earlier in this chapter, there are more germs in the mouth than the vagina or penis. The genitals need not be unpleasant to your sense of smell or taste. There are many good soaps today made from harmless vegetable-based ingredients that present a whole range of natural scents. Another idea that some people enjoy is massaging with scented, pleasant-tasting oils. Others use food, but take care which foods you use. Make sure they are not going to irritate the delicate genital tissues. In particular, beware of alcohol which can sting or even burn.

If your partner's discomfort with oral sex stems from an entrenched belief that it is morally 'wrong', then you must both be prepared to live with that conflict until you have overcome it. Your partner can expect to feel anxious and not quite right about it at first. But if you make the experience as pleasant as possible, and stop when she feels she has gone as far as she can, she will eventually be able to enjoy oral sex. While you are both working on it, make sure you include other ways of making love. Follow the suggestions in the answer to the first question in this chapter. Don't, whatever you do, try to have oral sex exclusively each time you make love.

Question

What *can* I do and what *can't* I do, from purely a safety aspect, when I give my girlfriend oral sex?

Answer

Obviously, do nothing that does physical harm to her,

and she will be the best judge of what hurts her. That aside, make sure your touching is gentle when she is not fully aroused and therefore lubricated. But once she reaches this state, more specific clitoral stimulation will probably be appropriate. Generally, any form of nuzzling, licking, sucking, stroking with your tongue, kissing, etc. is safe.

Question

I want to have oral sex with my husband, but I have developed this thing where I can't look at or touch his penis or scrotum. What is happening to me?

Answer

It's called an aversion, and you will overcome it gradually. It happens in a variety of sexual situations and could be included in almost any chapter because all aversions are dealt with in the same way. So that no matter whether you dislike looking at or touching a vagina or a penis, or the act of oral sex, the method of treating the aversion is the same.

First, try to explore the reason you have this particular aversion. While it will not solve your problem, it will help explain why you have problems in areas where the majority of people have very few.

Sometimes aversions disguise a distressing sexual experience which was pushed aside a long time ago. The types of experience we are talking about are usually more serious than a merely uncomfortable or embarrassing sexual encounter. Usually these have so deeply shocked the person that the only way he or she is able to deal with them is to totally block out what happened.

Unless there was encouragement and help to talk about it at the time, it will remain securely locked away until something such as an aversion arises. If this has happened to you, you will need to read Chapter 11 before continuing with this.

Another reason for aversions to sexual matters can stem from a very strict and therefore, restrictive, upbringing where anything to do with sex was taboo: no discussion, no answers to questions, no reference to it at all, except perhaps in the negative. Once again, we are not talking about the 'normal' embarrassment or discomfort with regard to sex that happens in most families when you are growing up.

A very severe religious background can also be responsible for producing the difficulties that lead to aversion. If you have experienced problems when you were growing up such as a strict religious background, or a totally negative attitude to sex, you will have to deal with that first, before tackling your present particular aversion.

What we are about to say may pleasantly surprise you, but dealing with an aversion need not be so difficult, nor does it have to include professional help. However, you will need an understanding and sympathetic person with whom you can talk.

If a sympathetic ear isn't available, try writing down your feelings. Writing out the facts of a problem has had very positive results for a lot of people. Expect to feel very upset, particularly if you had put out of your mind how difficult your upbringing was.

Try to draw conclusions about the past influences on your present reactions. However, if you are unable to come to any conclusions, don't let it worry you. You should find that just writing down or talking about the event or events of your past will help you express all your pent-up feelings. This will help you come to terms with those past problems.

It's better to take your time and not rush through this step. Remember, this will not overcome your aversion, it's simply the first step.

Should you feel that the above does not apply to your reason for an aversion, skip it and move on to the following procedure. It's essential that you have a co-operative partner for this part. We deal with penis aversion below. If your aversion is to oral sex or the vagina the steps are the same.

Steps To Take Together

1 Get yourselves comfortable in a relaxed atmosphere.
2 Lie down naked together and begin to talk generally about everyday matters. When you feel happy in each other's company, you can start to just look at your partner's penis.
3 If you feel very uncomfortable, end the session at the point where you have the most discomfort.
4 Repeat the above until you are able to look at his penis for longer and longer periods of time.
5 Once you have reached this stage, start touching his penis with your hands. This is only meant to familiarise you with its feel, it's not meant to be sexually arousing. While you are doing this ask him how he feels and what he likes. Stop at this point for this session.

(Practise steps one to five for a number of days or weeks until you feel comfortable. Should it take you longer than a couple of weeks then it is probably a good idea to seek professional guidance.)
Now you are ready to move on to the next steps.

6 Become more sexual with your touching, at all times maintaining some sort of communication with your partner, either verbal or non-verbal.
7 Make sure you have discussed a clear signal that conveys you want to stop, or change something you are doing.

8 Continue to make time together for these exercises, gradually pushing yourself further and further each time, but making sure you feel reasonably comfortable with one stage before progressing to the next.

9 If you want to go ahead with oral sex at this point, work out some steps that will bring you gradually closer and closer to having it. You could start by kissing your partner's genitals. Then you could stroke them, before returning to the kissing, gradually building up the time you kiss them. Eventually, move on to taking them in your mouth, or whatever your partner finds arousing. However, only arrive at this last stage by the same gradual steps of familiarisation as previously followed, until you are able to spend the amount of time necessary to stimulate and arouse your partner to orgasm through oral sex.

You must both be patient with this process. No one changes a lifetime's behaviour overnight. However, by the same token, staying too long on the one stage will mean you stand still and get nowhere. Don't stay at one stage for months on end with no progress. If this happens then you will both need to go to a clinical psychologist for a bit of help to move on to the next stage.

Question

I'm finding that I can perform oral sex on my husband, but he doesn't seem to want to do it for me. He is very old-fashioned in his attitude. When we have intercourse it only lasts for two minutes, including everything. I don't have an orgasm with him.

When I masturbate there is no problem with arousal and orgasm. Oral sex brings me to orgasm quicker than anything, and that is the reason I would like him to include it in our lovemaking. I enjoy it, too.

Before we married we made love quite often. I became used to this, but now weeks go by in between sex. It is a frustrating situation, and I am finding it very hard to cope with. Can you offer any advice?

Answer

There seem to be several things wrong in your relationship at the moment, quite apart from oral sex. You need to discuss with your husband frequency of sex, how to arouse you to orgasm and the inclusion of different sexual techniques. He is probably not being intentionally unco-operative. It may be that you have just not stated what you need clearly enough. You may also need to start initiating sex yourself more often. However, until both of you start discussing things, oral sex won't be the only unsatisfactory event in your life. Your whole relationship will be unsatisfactory.

Listeners Share Experiences

Oral sex has brought us closer together. At first it was not very good. My girlfriend's teeth got in the way, and she never pulled back my foreskin. It was all too awkward. Apparently I wasn't much better for her.

This may sound weird, but we talked about it at the football one day, after I blurted out: 'Is oral sex any good for you?'. I had been rehearsing it for a week.

I think we were just so generally up-tight about it, but wanting to please each other, so continued making a mess of it. It was like a watershed, and made it much easier to talk about other things in our sex life that we like or dislike.

My fiancée of three years will only have oral sex because she doesn't want to lose her virginity before

our wedding night. We have done everything but had intercourse, and have a lot of sex together. It seems hypocritical to me. I often wonder if I will be able to make her come when we do have intercourse. She has no problem having an orgasm at present.

My boyfriend is only interested in me having oral sex with him. There is no kissing, or touching or holding. Sex is becoming loathsome. There is not a scrap of pleasure in it for me.

My boyfriend won't show any affection for me. All he wants to do is have oral sex. Sometimes I want him so badly just to hold me. I tell him, but he really doesn't listen. It is not satisfying at all for me. He gets his pleasure, but I don't get mine. I love him, but I don't think the relationship has much of a future. He is obsessed with oral sex.

I want to know how to get my girlfriend involved in oral sex. I find it frustrating that she will not do it. She does everything else that I like. We've been going out for ten weeks now, and I just can't believe it is not happening yet. She's 27 and says she hasn't had much experience with men. I find it weird that at her age she is so inhibited.

My husband won't just make love, he wants oral sex all the time. He waits in bed for me at night, so I sit up for as long as I can, hoping he will fall asleep. I have even put sleeping tablets in his drinks at night on some occasions. I find oral sex revolting. And he just goes on and on and on with it. Maybe I should take the sleeping tablets because it has been a long time since I've had a good night's sleep. I don't know how much longer I can take this.

My girlfriend will let me go oral with her, but she

won't go oral with me. I find it extremely frustrating because I want to know how it would feel. She refuses pointblank to do it.

I have a wonderful relationship, made more wonderful by the discovery of oral sex. We are both in our seventies and only met recently, but in such a short time we have probably had the best sex of our lives. He is legally blind, but otherwise as fit as a fiddle.

Oral sex was just not right for me, morally or physically, in other relationships — including two marriages with children. Now it is as if a veil has been lifted, and it is the most natural thing in the world. I think giving my new man pleasure with it makes me feel very good about it. Guiding him when he does it to me is no problem either. It is a pity this has come so late in life, but we rarely worry about that, rather we just enjoy what we've got. I could never discuss it with people I know, more's the pity for them.

Chapter Eight

Pregnancy and Sex

There are some people in our society who still believe that pregnancy is what sex is all about. For them, one must not have sex without the intention of getting pregnant. And then there are others who believe that once a woman is pregnant, she no longer feels sexual — after all, she is pregnant isn't she?

The reality is that the majority of humans rarely have sex to make a baby, and a woman can't deny her need for sex just because she is pregnant.

Another common misapprehension about pregnancy and sex is that it could be harmful to the foetus if you continue to have sex during pregnancy. We will deal with this in more detail in the answer to a listener's query, later in this chapter.

Unfortunately, pregnancy *can* put a strain on a relationship. Sometimes the trouble can even begin before the woman gets pregnant. Just trying to have a baby can make for problems. Some couples get so wound up in trying to have sex 'at the right time' that they lose their perspective on the sexual relationship. They become like two prize breeding animals, with their sexual relationship reduced to thermometers, graphs, timing and constant intercourse.

Carrying on like this for any length of time will ensure that the sexual relationship becomes boring with a capital 'B'. You must guard against going over the top in this way. If you become this up-tight about conceiving, your chances may diminish. Whereas, if you put your emphasis on the enjoyment of the relationship and, as part of that, of your sexual relationship, then pregnancy probably won't be a problem.

However, if you fail to conceive after months of trying, then you may both need to consider fertility tests. If this is the case, then even through these more difficult circumstances, your enjoyment of sex should come first. By placing a high priority on your relationship it will help you both withstand the considerable stresses of trying to conceive in this way.

Many couples now, after bitter experience, have suffered the consequences of not putting their relationship before conception. The more emphasis you place on conception, and the more stress you put on your relationship, the more likely it will be that one of you finds everything too much to cope with and starts emotionally withdrawing.

While advances in fertility research have brought us some marvellous benefits, we feel that relationships have been pushed a little to one side.

There are many couples who can date the difficulties in their marriage from the time of having their first child. Of course, a new baby causes stresses and strains that test any relationship, but often the way in which the couple has gone about conceiving the baby has put excessive, negative pressure on the sexual relationship.

An over-emphasis on the importance of pregnancy can, in effect, be saying to a partner, 'The only worthwhile thing you can do for me as an individual is to give me a baby', or 'The only worthwhile thing we can do as a couple is to produce a baby'.

Clearly, relationships offer a lot more than babies. But if yours does not, perhaps you need to reconsider the relationship. Most certainly you need to reconsider having a baby. An attitude like this begins before the baby is born and continues throughout the birth, childhood and adolescence of this new life you have created.

Women must ask themselves if they really want to keep putting their partners second to their baby in all circumstances. If the answer is yes, they will probably eventually lose their partners. Not only that, but they will lose one of the most important people in their child's life — his or her father.

Perhaps it needs to be clearly stated at this point that we are not advocating neglectful parenthood, nor are we suggesting that single parents can't survive very well alone. However, most people would still agree that, where possible, two parents are preferable to one.

So be careful when you plan to have a baby that you don't insist your partner has sex on a particular night if she or he is tired, sick or just not feeling sexy. Waiting a few months to conceive won't matter if it ensures you don't drive your partner out of the relationship.

If you have decided to have children, then both sit down and discuss your feelings about it. Include in the discussion issues such as: to what lengths you are prepared to go to have the baby; whether or not you have the resources, particularly emotional resources, to cope when the baby arrives; and the management of the baby, that is, how to divide your time making sure that each of you has time to yourself, and time when you give the relationship high priority. This may be the kind of planning you would associate with a major expedition, or making a large investment, but having a baby is a much bigger event than either of these. There can be a good deal of tension and uncertainty surrounding having a baby, and this type of planning and discussion will help alleviate some of it.

Some of the most distressing calls we took on radio were from women who were pregnant, close to having their babies, and whose husbands or boyfriends were obviously rapidly losing interest in the relationship. There was a chilling callousness about the attitude of the male partner. This must be one of the most awful situations to which a pregnant woman could be subjected: to discover her relationship was not working at the very time she needed all the help and support she could get — especially from the father of her child.

The saddest part of such situations was that they could have been avoided, had the couple talked seriously about having a child. They could have decided whether or not the relationship was able to cope with a pregnancy long before they had the responsibility of another life on their doorstep.

A discussion of the issues outlined above (whether or not you have the financial and emotional resources, etc., to cope with a baby) can also help a couple facing an unplanned pregnancy to sort out their feelings and priorities. Ideally, this should be done with the help of a qualified counsellor. If the woman finds she wants to continue with the pregnancy, but the man feels he is unable to cope with parenthood, it can be better for them to part. Despite the initial upset, they can then both feel that — given the circumstances — they have made the right decision. This is a much less traumatic situation than the one where a couple stay together because it is the done thing. Inevitably, they would become increasingly distressed as the pregnancy progressed.

There are two common situations in which expectant parents can find themselves. In one, the couple overemphasise pregnancy at the cost of the relationship, and, in the other, the couple take it so lightly that virtually no plans are made — this also leads to major difficulties for the relationship. Both situations occur too often for comfort.

A woman who is planning to become pregnant or who has an unplanned pregnancy should ask herself the following questions.

- Is my relationship my top priority?
- If so, am I prepared to fully take into account the feelings of my partner?
- Am I prepared to keep pregnancy and eventual parenthood in perspective, or am I going to wilfully disregard the cost to the relationship and my partner's thoughts and feelings?
- Am I prepared to put enjoyment in our sexual relationship at the top of my list?

BEFORE YOU GET PREGNANT

A final general word about parenthood today. It seems to be fashionable to treat pregnancy and the birth of a baby as an event that should make little or no difference to your lifestyle. This is glossing over the true facts. Being pregnant and then having a baby will make a BIG difference to your life. Plan and try to anticipate the changes with which you will have to cope, rather than deny the facts of this new life. Bringing another human being into the world is a wonderful event which should be sufficiently catered for, both emotionally and physically.

Forget the fashionable attitude of 'and baby makes three, with no difference at all'. Don't be tempted by the idea of being a SUPER COUPLE who keep up all their old activities after having a baby.

While everyone else may think you are marvellous, only you will know the high price you are paying to keep up these appearances.

The rule of thumb is to cut back on your activities, interests and work and focus on your relationship and family. If this raises doubts for you, then perhaps you need to consider remaining as you are — without children.

TIPS ON BECOMING PREGNANT

The following tips may help couples to conceive — and at the same time protect their relationships.

1 Get into perspective the length of time it should take to become pregnant. Don't expect it to happen the first month that you try. After stopping contraception, give yourself six to maybe even twelve months. As there are only a small number of fertile days in each woman's cycle it is not always easy to be sexually interested at the right time. It is important to heed your doctor's orders if he or she advises at least one or two periods after coming off the Pill. Use other contraception during this time.

2 It could be an added advantage for the woman to learn to recognise her signs of fertility, observing bodily secretions as per the Billings method (see Recommended Reading). Then she could initiate sex when she knew she was likely to conceive. However, at no time should the couple make this into a 'do-or-die' effort. 'We MUST have sex tonight', is an attitude which puts on the pressure that can often produce the opposite effect for a couple. Besides, a woman remains fertile for a number of days, so simply try again the next day if neither of you are in the mood at first.

3 Plan plenty of time to have your baby and get back to your job so that you don't feel pressured to do it all within, say, a year.

4 A top relaxation trick is to focus on enjoying your relationship. Even though there is no hard evidence for this, you will both feel better and probably conceive more easily if you are relaxed — relaxed in your attitude to your life in general and particularly to the idea of conceiving.

5 If your relationship is rocky, spend time working on it before becoming pregnant.

6 Don't spend every month hoping that it will be the one in which you finally conceive. Say to yourself, 'I will give myself the best possible chance to become pregnant, but there are other things that are important to me, particularly my relationship'.

In the answers to the following questions we discuss issues which were often raised by listeners on the subject of sex and pregnancy.

Question

Is it risky to the foetus to have sex when you are pregnant? Just how safe is it?

Answer

Men usually ask this question. Their concern is that intercourse will in some way damage the foetus.

This fear is based on lack of knowledge about the structure of a woman's body. The vagina and womb (or uterus) are separate. Not only this, but the neck of the womb, which is called the cervix, is a very tightly closed muscle. When a woman is pregnant, the cervix is totally blocked to protect the foetus, which in turn prevents anything getting into the womb. Nothing that enters the vagina can get through the cervix, so there is absolutely no risk of damage to the foetus during sexual intercourse.

Given normal circumstances, sex should present no problem. However, where there is a particular medical condition, a doctor may advise the couple not to have intercourse.

A word here about doctors and pregnancy. Couples are often intimidated into silent submission when a doctor advises against sex. They don't like to appear to be questioning his or her expertise. However, they may be left in the dark about why the suggestion was made. Remember that anyone who gives advice, even in a professional capacity, is only human. They are still ruled by their own beliefs and values, which might have no scientific basis. Doctors should be aware of this and be able to let the patient know the difference between a personal opinion and a scientific or medical fact. As this does not always happen, you must be the judge of whether or not a doctor's advice is medical fact. If he or she has difficulty discussing this, seek a second opinion.

Question

I feel as much like having sex now that I am pregnant as I did before I was carrying the baby. Is this normal?

Answer

Women who are interested in sex throughout their pregnancy are probably women who are confident about their sexuality, and have knowledge about what happens to their bodies during pregnancy. If a woman has been active and interested in sex before, then there is no reason to assume this will change with pregnancy, as long as she gets sufficient rest and relaxation.

It is important that a couple makes a big issue of relaxation in their lives at this time to preserve the relationship as a whole, and the sexual relationship in particular. The woman must spend enough time resting, and not be placed under stress, and they must both spend sufficient time just being together in a relaxed, enjoyable way.

It is true that during certain stages of pregnancy a woman won't be interested in sex. There can be many

118

reasons for this. In the early stages she may feel nauseous and tired, and in the later stages she may feel big and heavy and just not sexy.

Then there are the women who report increased interest in sex. They also say they have an increased ability to become aroused and reach orgasm. This is quite possibly due to the increased blood flow to the pelvic area.

Question

I'm worried about whether or not it is safe to wear a tampon while I'm pregnant. I hate waking up in a mess in the morning after I have had sex, so I insert a tampon and leave it there overnight. Is this okay?

Answer

This is not a good idea. The recommended length of time you should leave a tampon inserted is three to four hours. Overnight is much too long. Get up and wash if you are concerned about semen in the bed. If you find it too uncomfortable to be hauling yourself out of bed, or it breaks the mood after you have made love, have a damp towel or tissues beside the bed and use these.

Question

Can we continue to have sex late into pregnancy?

Answer

Yes. There is no reason to stop your sexual relationship at this stage. However, if your doctor has advised against it, question him or her on the medical facts of the advice. As we have said previously, some doctors still recommend suspending sexual intercourse without any medical evidence that it is harmful. Of course, if your doctor is able to give you a satisfactory reason, then don't have intercourse, but this does not mean you have to stop your sexual relationship. As discussed earlier, sex is more than just intercourse.

Some couples believe, or are led to believe, that if a woman has an orgasm late in pregnancy it will bring on labour. There is no conclusive evidence on this. On the other hand, there are women who say it has happened to them. The reason is more likely to be that they had reached the end of their pregnancy anyway. In no way can orgasm or intercourse be shown to be responsible for premature births or miscarriages.

Later in a pregnancy, a woman may feel uncomfortable having intercourse. This can be overcome by changing intercourse positions so that there is no pressure on her stomach and she can control the depth of penetration. There are two positions that are particularly good: the couple lying side by side, or the woman sitting above her partner who is lying down. Both these positions are possible to use until the end of pregnancy.

If you are both feeling tired and worn out, mutual massage is a good alternative. There are many things you can do together that are sensual or affectionate that are not intercourse, but will maintain the bonds in your relationship. Even sitting together holding hands listening to music can be a tonic.

Question

Since I've been carrying my second baby, I've become a raving sex maniac — at least that's what my husband's calling me. Poor old bloke. I think he's having trouble keeping up. But he is also surprised, as am I, because it was the furthest thing from my mind with my first. Why?

Answer

No two pregnancies are the same and you are obviously an excellent example of this. The whole area around the vagina gets a larger supply of blood while you are pregnant and this is usually the reason for increased interest. Orgasms probably occur more easily as well. Make sure your 'poor old bloke' isn't having trouble coming to terms with a sexier-feeling mother-to-be on his hands. If he is happy, go ahead! There is nothing harmful in a more frequent sexual relationship while you are pregnant.

Question

Why would my wife have gone off sex since the baby was born? It has been twelve months, and her response is still negative. She dismisses me, whenever I try to make overtures to her. It really makes me feel unwanted. We're otherwise very happy, and I honestly help her with everything. The baby has been a shared thing.

Answer

Here are some pointers to help you direct the conversation and discussions in a more positive direction, because you must get to the bottom of this.

- Clearly tell her how important your sexual relationship is to you, and how badly her dismissal of you and her refusal to discuss things affects you.
- Get specific reasons for her lack of interest. Is it something she dislikes? Is she tired, despite your help? Is she getting enough time with you, just enjoying your company, without having the baby around? Is her new

life with the baby something she is really happy about?
- Remember, when people feel bad about some part of their life this is often reflected in their sex life. This does not mean there is anything wrong with their sex life — that is just where the problem is manifesting itself.

You and your wife must work out where your particular problem is. You have come this far, in asking for help, so keep up the good work! Be very firm and straightforward with your wife.

Question

I am just so tired. My baby is four months old and I'm breastfeeding, getting plenty of rest periods and a lot of help from my husband and family. But I just can't get over the tiredness. My doctor says it will go away eventually. I don't feel like sex, and the doctor says that is because of the breastfeeding. This doesn't make sense to me, but I didn't ask the doctor for an explanation. What could he have meant?

Answer

Make sure you DO get the rest and help you need. There is a fair amount of suggestion from research that breastfeeding can make a woman less interested in sex because of the hormone that circulates while this is going on. However, it is a complicated argument because it relies on the fact that one hormone is affecting a whole learned pattern of behaviour, which is highly unlikely. It is more likely that fatigue and the demands of caring for the baby have dulled your interest in sex. It is most important that you and your husband discuss this situation, and agree on alternatives to intercourse, such as cuddling, to show you are still important to each other. As long as you give each other affection and understanding, your interest in sex will resume when you feel more energetic.

Question

How long should we wait to resume intercourse after the baby is born?

Answer

If you thought the discomfort and fatigue of pregnancy were a test of your patience and love for each other 'you ain't seen nothin' yet!'. The sexual relationship is under the most strain after your baby is born. Up until now you have probably been able to compensate for the lack of passion with affectionate and sensual behaviour. Even this could be too much to ask once your baby comes along.

The key to managing this difficult period is time set aside for both of you. More about that in a moment.

To answer your question: it is safe to resume sex within two weeks of the birth. Some doctors still say six weeks, but it is generally agreed that the cervix has completely closed again at two weeks. If, however, the woman had some trauma associated with the birth, such as stitches or a forceps delivery, the resulting bruising could make intercourse painful. Bruising and swelling can take some time to heal.

If this happens, you can mutually masturbate one another as part of your sexual interaction rather than rushing into intercourse that feels uncomfortable.

Generally, during the first two weeks, and up to the time you are ready for intercourse, focus on re-establishing the affectionate, sensual side of your relationship. Don't put all your affection and time into the care of baby, leave some time and energy for one another.

If your relationship is important to you, then you *must* spend time together relaxing and doing things for your pleasure. Sex will suffer if you rush around looking after the baby, your house, your job or your family, leaving only a minute amount of time for you as a couple. You would also be so exhausted that all you would want to do would be sleep.

Ideally, both of you should cut back on work for a little while. Make sure there is time, every day, to sit and relax over dinner or just to spend alone with each other at the end of the day. Go out at least once a week, on your own.

Don't sacrifice your relationship for the sake of the baby. The alternative can be a bitter, lonely one — your baby being the child of a single parent family, with the other parent only given visiting rights.

To sum up: it is safe to resume sex two weeks after birth. If you have had any trauma at birth, wait until the bruising and swelling disappear and sex is comfortable. Give your sex life its correct priority. Make time to enjoy each other.

Should intercourse still be painful after three months immediately seek medical advice.

Question

We were married for six years before we had children. There was no problem in our sex life during those days, in fact it was great. We were able to talk with each other about it. After the children things changed quite rapidly — the reverse now applies. I've come to the conclusion I could quite happily do without sex for the rest of my life. My husband seems

to have different needs to mine. Where I would be quite satisfied with a kiss and a cuddle, he seems to think if he has a cuddle he has to perform.

Answer

You must try to get back to talking, because you need to explore a lot more about each other in terms of what you want from sex. As you have not talked, you may find that sex has changed for him too, and he is simply doing what he thinks is right. Like your taste in food, sex is an ever-changing part of your life. Find out if both, or either, of you are after more time together — having had children your time would be divided more ways — or if you just want to be closer, or more intimate. Often the man will keep initiating sex when he really just wants more time with his wife (see also Chapter 6).

Listeners Share Experiences

We have been trying to have a baby for eleven years. In that time we have been to about five specialists, but it was only the last one who diagnosed my wife as having endometriosis (the growth of the endometrium outside the womb). It was blocking the neck of the womb. Surgery took care of it and we are very hopeful that she will now conceive. The gynaecologist says there shouldn't be any problems. So to anyone trying to get pregnant, I just want to say don't give up, and don't be afraid to change your specialist.

I am scared my husband will go to another woman for sex. I'm eight months pregnant and he still requires as much sex as we had before I got pregnant. I am not feeling very comfortable right now, but I usually give in to him. If I stopped having inter-

course with him I think I would be robbing him of his sexual pleasure.

When I have tried to explain how uncomfortable intercourse is for me he has looked a little upset and expressed annoyance at the situation. It reminds me of times before I was pregnant when I would put on a little bit of extra weight and felt that I was unattractive to him. I am really worried he will go looking for another woman.

Chapter Nine

Sex as You Get Older

We could open this chapter by citing examples of famous people for whom age has not meant a lessening of vitality, involvement and general interest in life, and say this is the way it can be for you too. However, the people we wish to draw to your attention, to salute and to thank here, are the not-so-famous: our older listeners.

They were superb. They called the program in their hundreds during our five years together on air, and generously related their experiences and philosophies. Most of them also had a great capacity to learn anything new, anything that could be helpful to their enjoyment of life.

Some, of course, had sad stories; others had surprising ones. There was the 86-year-old widow who had erotic dreams about her late husband; the newly-widowed man whose sex life had been the more exciting because he and his wife had had separate bedrooms; the couples in their fifties, newly-released from child-raising, who were finally able to concentrate on each other, and find a new joy in their sexual relationships.

One of the most famous guests on our program, American comedian Phyllis Diller, must have given heart to many of our older (and younger) listeners when she said she still got goosebumps at the sight of a good-looking man. She was 70 years old at the time!

While she admitted to a string of male friends, scattered across America, there was one special man with whom she had an exclusive sexual relationship.

Explaining, 'I'd rather talk about your subject than anything else in the world', she opened up on what Phyllis Diller was like when in love.

'I like to make love, I like to have candlelight and wine, travel and social activity, warm beaches and a tender breeze, moonlight, and all that stuff.'

And of sex and her age she said, 'I have had a wonderful time. I've had a very sexy life and I hope it continues. I think it is terribly good for you. One of the most helpful things people can have in their lives is good sex.'

Examples, like Phyllis Diller's, of life lived fully into the seventies and beyond may one day be par for the course. 'One day' because despite an improvement in attitude to older people — with better health care and special education programs for the aged — there is still a general feeling in our community that when someone retires from a job he or she also retires from normal life.

Unfortunately, because of such social attitudes, many older people deny their own sexuality, believing it is inappropriate for them to show any interest in sex. This is particularly noticeable in people who lose a partner. They are often reluctant to seek out further companionship, possibly due to an uncertainty about how to make new friends.

Research shows that women are more likely to remain alone than men. This is possibly because there are more older women than men, and also because men tend to seek out younger partners. Also, women may be more inhibited about getting into new relationships. Whatever the reasons, more education and information are needed, so people have the opportunity to express themselves sexually throughout their lives, regardless of age.

It is worth remembering that if people have been sexually active well into middle age they will probably continue to take an active interest in sex as they grow older. The expression of this sexuality may take different forms, but the interest will still be there.

Of course, as people become older they may have to cope with physical problems that could interfere, to a certain extent, with their sexual expression. Ideally, there should be more aid and counselling available to help people overcome such difficulties. However, poor health and old age need not prevent people from enjoying sexual activities.

PHYSICAL CHANGES THAT OCCUR AS YOU GET OLDER

The main change is that all systems slow down. The body no longer functions as efficiently as it did. But this change is very gradual, and if a person is healthy it is easy to adapt. In terms of a sexual relationship, this slower pace is often an advantage.

Of course, the most obvious changes to older people occur in their outward appearance: to their faces and bodies. The myth still pervades in our culture that someone has to *look* sexually attractive — that is, to conform to the stereotype of being slim, smooth-muscled and young — to *be* sexually attractive. This has strong negative influences on older people. Accepting this myth, they resign themselves to no further sexual satisfaction. Sometimes it is a bitter resignation.

Another negative attitude in our society towards old people is that we tend to regard them as ill people. And we then draw the conclusion that they can't be interested in, or capable of, a sexual relationship. This is a long way from reality.

There are ways of coping with the physical changes of ageing, which we will discuss further. But the psychological changes, which have usually become entrenched very early in a person's life, are the most damaging and difficult to overcome. In order to do so, you have to be prepared for a head-on clash with the negative influences that have encouraged you to sit back and avoid further sexual relationships.

It is not easy. You must challenge the myth that to be sexually active you need to be young, that because your body has physically aged, you can't be attractive to another person. In fact, it would be helpful for people of all ages to challenge these myths.

It is a tribute to some older people that, despite lack of encouragement, they have been able to overcome the opposition and have developed healthy, satisfying sexual relationships. To these people, researchers and psychologists owe a debt. The information they have provided enables health professionals to encourage and help other older people follow in their footsteps and develop their own rewarding sexual relationships.

Here are the physical changes you can expect gradually to take place as you age.

MALES

1 Lower levels of testosterone, which bring decreased fertility (fewer sperm), weakening of the cardiovascular and immune systems, muscle tone and general strength.
2 The testes become smaller and more flaccid.
3 The prostate gland enlarges, which brings weaker contractions at orgasm and corresponding change in sensation at ejaculation.

4 The force of ejaculation is decreased. (These first four changes are partly responsible for changes in feeling and sensation during sex as you age.)
5 Excitement builds more slowly, with direct stimulation of the penis often needed.
6 Erections are less firm and there is less testicular elevation.
7 Penile circumference increases, but there is no pre-ejaculatory fluid as in younger years.
8 Orgasm is shorter — one or two contractions compared with the three or four of youth.
9 Loss of erection after ejaculation takes only a few seconds, and older males may have to wait for 12 to 24 hours before another erection is possible.

FEMALES

1 Lower oestrogen levels, which correspond with menopause, may bring some uncomfortable physical symptoms: reduction in skin elasticity, decreased muscle tone, fatty tissue redistribution and sagging breasts.
2 Fertility decreases.
3 The mons flattens and the major labia are less full.
4 The cervix, uterus and ovaries grow smaller. In some they may reach pre-pubertal size.
5 Vaginal walls thin and become less elastic.
6 Lubrication can diminish, but if tissue is maintained by healthy sexual activity (intercourse or masturbation) it is often sufficient.
7 The clitoris reduces in size, but there is little change in sensitivity.
8 Urogenital problems can occur as a result of the changes, making a woman more susceptible to

vaginal infections that could lead to pain at intercourse. Medication and following a doctor's advice can overcome this.

9 Vasocongestion of genitals diminishes and lubrication, while present or possible, takes longer: anywhere between 15 and 30 seconds to as much as five minutes.

10 Clitoral functioning is the same, although the lips of the vagina do not fill out during arousal as they did.

11 Contractions at orgasm are reduced and less rhythmic.

12 Return to the pre-arousal phase occurs very quickly.

These physical changes that occur in both sexes inevitably create corresponding changes in the nature of a sexual relationship. There is less emphasis on climax and intercourse, and more on the sensuality of interacting bodily with another person. Warmth and intimacy take on more importance than achieving sexual gratification. The mature sexual relationship can, in many ways, be more rewarding and stimulating than the comparatively quicker intercourse and climax of younger lovers.

Just because sexual response slows down, it does not mean *feelings* of sexual interest diminish. These feelings can remain for as long as we live. They will be maintained if a person has always been sexually active.

It is interesting to note that when it comes to the physical changes of old age, women seem to be left with the sexual advantage over men, because their ability to reach orgasm and have multiple orgasms is not impaired by age.

ILLNESS AND MEDICATION

Although many older people remain healthy and fit into old age, many others may suffer from some sort of chronic illness requiring medication. Either the illness or the medication can have side-effects that create problems with sexual ability. Here are some of the more common physical problems and side-effects.

HYPERTENSION

Sexual activity among hypertensive males seems to be severely decreased and even absent. It is uncertain whether the problem is due to lack of sexual interest resulting from the sedative effects of the drugs taken, or because the drugs somehow interfere with the mechanical ability of an erection. This response seems to vary with the individual. Generally, though, there are men who fear sex when they have any sort of illness, as if failure to perform is inevitable. Some hypertensives avoiding sex could fall into this category.

DIABETES

Almost 50 per cent of men and women diabetics report sexual disability, despite a quite healthy interest in sex. Mainly for the females, the problem is lack of lubrication; and for the males, either impotence, or premature or retrograde ejaculation. The reasons males have these problems when they become diabetic are twofold: the arterial blood supply to the penis is gradually cut off by calcification, which narrows blood vessels; and the nerves that take care of the smooth muscle, which controls the erection of the penis, deteriorate.

CARDIOVASCULAR DISEASE

There is no justification for a person with cardiovascular disease avoiding sex, unless specifically advised against it by a doctor. The physical effort of sex is only equivalent to moderate exercise, which most doctors prescribe for these patients. Having sex can also reduce emotional and physical tension, which in turn improves outlook. However, to be on the safe side, you should ask your doctor if sex is a risk for you.

PELVIC SURGERY

Pelvic surgery seems to have a drastic effect on men and women's sexuality. It is often used as an excuse for abstinence. However, research shows that 80 per cent of males who have had prostates removed retain their ability to have an erection and 70 per cent of hysterectomy patients are still able to achieve orgasm. Once again, the effects vary with the individual, but usually they are more related to the psychological than the physical problems.

Pre-surgery discussion is very important for the continued sexual well-being of a person. It should clearly establish the facts about whether the surgery will interfere with sexual ability. In most cases it will not. These discussions should also include the person's partner so that they can work out their fears and concerns before the operation.

MASTECTOMY

An operation that outwardly scars a person can in itself be devastating, without the additional fear of cancer and death that mastectomy brings. Add to this our preoccupation with breasts being perfect, pert symbols of sexuality, and one can understand just how extraordinarily difficult it can be to cope with a mastectomy. The fear of being rejected and the concern about still being loved get mixed up with coping with such major surgery. Expert counselling before the operation and plenty of support and follow-up counselling are a must with mastectomy.

A loving and sexual relationship is the perfect antidote to illness or physical disability. Everyone benefits. It may not be as passionately intense as it was early on, but it will almost certainly provide intimacy and a sense of sharing that become more and more rewarding.

Young people reading this may not believe that a quiet, intimate relationship could be sexually satisfying. However, encouraged to maintain a healthy sexual relationship throughout their young and middle years, they will discover this wonderful stage of life where physical problems and disabilities are of small consequence compared with the closeness of two devoted people.

DEVELOPING AND MAINTAINING SEXUAL CAPACITY

Ideally, people should be encouraged from an early age to view themselves as sexual throughout life and be made to realise that their sexuality will last, in some form, until the day they die. They also need to broaden their understanding of sexuality to include all sorts of people of varying ages. Then perhaps our narrow and limiting stereotype of a sexy person being young and active would disappear.

If this advice seems a little late, if you are already into old age and have not had such an ideal sexual education, then don't despair! The next best thing is for you to have access to a helpful and understanding counsellor with experience in dealing with sexuality in older age: a person who is not going to make you feel uncomfortable because you are old and asking about sex; someone who can answer your specific problems and help you enjoy your sex life.

Our radio program often fulfilled this function, although it was a drop in the ocean compared with the need for information that older people had. As with other age-groups and problems, it was surprising just how basic the questions were. If only, years ago, someone had answered their simple queries they would not have spent so much time feeling upset and worried about whatever they saw as a problem, a stumbling-block to their sexual satisfaction.

Medical research could play a larger part in maintaining sexual capacity for older people. Maybe there are drugs that can be developed to help medical problems which don't interfere with sexuality. Perhaps medical and other health professionals could do more to educate people to develop lifestyles that would enable them to remain fit and capable into their old age.

DISAPPROVAL FROM 'THE CHILDREN'

In this so-called enlightened age many older couples who begin sexual relationships with new partners are worried about what their adult offspring think. In some recent research it was reported that most adult 'children' reacted negatively to their parents forming a new relationship, being embarrassed and upset by the obvious sexual nature of the relationship.

This was confirmed by many of our older callers, who felt that they had to prevent their new partner and adult offspring meeting because of this disapproval. This situation, more than anything, points to our general lack of acceptance of sexuality in old age.

One of our listeners, a lively lady of 80, described this

negative reaction from adult offspring as 'the generation gap in reverse'. Her comments are quoted in full at the end of this chapter.

HOW TO COPE WHEN ONE PARTNER IS ILL

A distressing difficulty arises when one partner is very ill — perhaps terminally — and the other is fit and healthy. We had a number of callers who were either in this situation or had been through it.

The difficulty is to meet the needs of both partners. The one who is ill needs companionship, warmth and intimacy as well, of course, as nursing and care. The healthy partner also needs support and companionship but, at the same time, may still be interested in social events, having fun, and a sexual relationship.

One very courageous couple solved this problem in a creative way: first, by discussing the inevitability of the husband's death; secondly, by recognising that he would feel increasingly unwell and uninterested in doing many things with his wife; and thirdly, by recognising that she had a right to her own life, that she should not just spend all her time with him. He was able to allow his wife her independence, yet at the same time she willingly spent a lot of time with her husband. Eventually, she became involved with another man and their relationship became sexual, but she was able to share this with her husband. In the end this other man also established a friendship with her husband, and the three of them remained firm friends until the husband's death.

A better example of intimacy and sharing could not be found anywhere. It must, at times, have been extremely difficult for this husband and wife to face such a devastating situation. But they not only faced it, they gained something worthwhile out of it. They demonstrated that relating to another person and being intimate with someone isn't about owning that person and making them suffer with you, it's about being able to let them be free to choose what they will do. The wife never, despite her attachment to the other man, contemplated leaving her husband. And, despite the hurt and pain, the couple's relationship was apparently better than ever when the husband died.

Obviously, this solution isn't for everyone. It has to be up to individuals to work out what is right for them, but it is amazing what people can do if they try. The fear of the consequences of talking frankly often prevents people improving their lives. The woman discussed in this example must have been eternally grateful for her husband's courage in raising the issue and encouraging her to establish a life of her own.

The following questions are typical of dozens we received from older listeners.

Question

I'm 65 years old and have been widowed for three years. I'd like to meet a man about my own age, but feel a bit shy about it. Am I too old?

Answer

As people get older, particularly if they have lost or divorced a partner, they stop seeing themselves as sexual beings. They close down that part of their lives, systematically avoiding meeting a new partner, and instead confine themselves to being a grandparent or a parent or just having a few friends. They think that their chance to find love is over. Nothing could be further from the truth.

You don't stop being sexual because you are older, any more than you stop getting hungry, or needing shelter. Your sex life need not be over, and you stand as good a chance as anyone younger of meeting a person and developing a loving relationship, if only you will take the time and apply yourself.

Anyone who has talked herself or himself into believing that older people don't need their own love lives, needs to seriously challenge this belief. He or she also needs to challenge the belief that sex is just for the young.

A young body is no guarantee of a successful sexual relationship. Older people who fall in love will find that they can feel just as sexy, romantic and loved as a young person, or indeed as they themselves did when they were in love with their first partner.

But you will never discover, or re-discover, this while you sit at home letting the years drift by. No matter how nervous and unsure you are of yourself, you must make yourself join clubs or organisations that interest you where you will take part in the activities and, at the same time, meet people of your own age.

Question

I have not had a regular sex partner for the past five years. However, I have had sex a few times and, each time I do, I get slight bleeding. My doctor has given me an internal examination and says everything is in good condition.

As I am now 70 I thought it might have to do with lubrication, but I was very aroused on each occasion I had sex. I saw an ad in *Cleo* for KY Jelly, but could not bring myself to go into a chemist shop and ask for it.

I thought I might cut out the advertisement, take it to a female chemist and just point at it. I'd feel less embarrassed if it went according to plan, but if she laughed I'd die. What do you think?

Answer

Love the idea. And yes, it is probably lubrication, or lack of it, making you bleed. Even though you were aroused on each occasion, because of your age you probably did not produce enough lubrication to handle the thrusting of your partner's penis. Also, the lining of the vagina gets thinner as you get older.

Question

I am an 86-year-old lady with a sex problem. Is it natural for me to feel sexual? I am having recurring dreams about my late husband. He is feeling my body. When I wake up it is my own hands rubbing my private parts, and I feel terrific. Do other old people feel this way or am I the only one? This does worry me.

Answer

It's perfectly natural. Your love for your husband must have been a wonderful deep emotion. If only more old people would acknowledge their sexuality you, and others like you, would not be experiencing that worry. Instead, you would be reaping the benefits of your years of experience, and you would feel sex was still just as much a natural part of your life as any other need.

140

Question

My husband has been terminally ill for eighteen months. I can tell he is worried about me being alone, but, unfortunately, I can't bring myself to discuss it. However, he becomes noticeably worse each day, and this worry hangs in the air.

Answer

There has been quite a lot of research done on dying partners that shows they usually feel concern for the future emotional and sexual needs of the spouse soon to be left alone.

Most expressed a preference for discussing this concern to help feel reassured that their partners would be all right after they had gone. Such discussion often relieved them of much worry. However, one of the reasons the lines of communication often remain shut is that the surviving spouse is afraid to speak frankly. Surprisingly, dying partners are quite willing to talk about the situation. Take the plunge, prefacing it with how difficult it is for you to raise the subject, but that you feel he wants to talk about it.

Question

When I enter my wife, I can move my penis for a little while, but then it goes limp. I'm 63, have had a water stoppage and prostate problems.

Answer

There is some work that suggests this is a physical problem. One solution is to change positions because it is to do with the blood flow to the penis. The movement shunts the blood out of the penis. So if your wife is underneath you when you enter her, try with her on top of you. If this does not work, it is essential you see a urologist.

Question

I find it difficult to keep an even balance in my life because my husband has been more than two years in a nursing home.

He had a stroke which has left him with a limited mental capacity. I recognise I must make a new life for myself, but I don't know how. I also think it is too soon, but I have such a strong need. I try to hide how I feel from the rest of the family because I don't want them to worry about me as well as him. The loneliness, depression and unhappiness are sometimes unbearable. What's your advice?

Answer

The balance you mention is extremely difficult to keep in your situation, but it is of paramount importance that you try to achieve it. Without it you won't cope. Therefore, starting to establish a life for yourself is most important — as you seem to recognise. Go to someone for help now. Try the voluntary helping agencies for families in the front of your phone book, a psychologist, or perhaps a counselling service attached to a hospital (see also Support Organisations). They should help you recognise that it is all right for you to start thinking about yourself as an individual with needs that can no longer be met by your partner, and show you how to go about setting up your life again.

You have the added pressure of not being able to discuss the problem with your husband. If one partner is not able to comprehend what is happening (for physical reasons) then the responsibility sits squarely on the shoulders of the well person to make decisions for himself or herself. Don't let the family stand in your way. If any of them carry on in an unreasonable way, you may have to be quite assertive, stating that it is your business and that you are not prepared to discuss it. Don't fall for the oft-touted 'It is an insult to his memory' line.

A final difficulty to consider is that you may take on too much by racing into another relationship then find that the balancing act of looking after your spouse and devoting time to the new person becomes too much to handle.

Listeners Share Experiences

I have met a man, after four years of divorce, and I am not at all confident about starting sex with him. I am in my fifties and it has been ten years since I had sex with a man, and he was my first and only love. I have tended to direct myself into good works or babysitting and have lost sight of myself as a sexual being.

I reckon that the best part of a couple's sexual relationship happens later in life, when the kids are gone. The late thirties were the hardest for us because we had no privacy.

The wife gave a good deal of her time to the children. I contributed but, like it or not, the bulk of that burden fell onto her shoulders.

I remember thinking to myself: 'Well, here I am in my late thirties, as fit as a bull. I should be having sex every night, because I'm not getting any younger'.

But it's got nothing to do with youth, it is to do with old age! So I'd just like to say to people in their child-rearing stage, if you can hang on until your mid-forties you've got a treat in store. It is beautiful!

My friend has a rod in his penis which gives him an erection. There is a little pump down by his testes that he uses to pump up his penis. He needed this device as the result of an accident (about six years ago) that damaged some of his nerves.

We think the pump has been a great success. The only drawback is that because he has a semi-erection all the time he is unable to get into bathers. We are in our sixties and he is a marvellous lover who has no trouble finding my G-spot!

I have a partner who is mentally as well as terminally ill. My moral obligation is to look after him. However, this leaves me living a very lonely and empty life. Why do I and others in the same situation with the same moral ties have to be starved of emotional outlet? Don't get me wrong, I am not complaining. I would never leave him while I could help him, that was the vow I took when we married, and I want to honour it. But I am rapidly realising how unhealthy it is for me to cut off my emotions, to not have someone with whom to express them sexually, affectionately and mentally. I particularly need it at this trying time.

When I hear what sex is really all about on your program I feel I should never have been let loose in my younger days. I didn't know a thing. The ones I went to school with must have been the same, or else they kept it to themselves.

I was nearly 12 when I started this monthly business, and hadn't been told anything about it. This day my bloomers got stained and I thought I'd cut my leg, so I got in the bath to wash away the blood. My mother and I were living with an aunt at the time. I got into bed, leaving the bloomers folded with a note on them about cutting my leg.

Of course, I got woken up and told what it was and that it would happen each month. I was *furious*. No *way* was it going to happen to me. I wasn't going to put up with that! But, of course, I had to learn to live with it. I often wondered if anyone else reacted towards their mother in such a way, at such a time.

I had no trouble starting friendships in the 1940s, and soon met my husband who was a little older than me, and a kind, gentle man. Sex wasn't a big thing with either of us; we could take it or leave it. As you two say, a touch, a look, or just holding hands and being good friends suited me just as well. I've been by myself for fifteen years now and think at times it makes you selfish in lots of ways: you do as you like when you like. But at times I think a man's company — and I mean company at my age — would be all right.

(This was from a regular listener, a wonderful 75-year-old woman.)

At 80, I'm ashamed to say, my sex drive is as strong as it ever was. I say 'ashamed' because I really feel that 80 is too old! However, what does one do when life presents you with such a dilemma?

I have to attribute it to my robust health. In the past thirty years I have not had one head-ache, nor have I had as much as a cold. My blood pressure has also been constant.

My man friend thinks I'm 65. He's 64.

Being active has always been important; I walk a lot and still run on occasion, so that I'm very slim.

My daughters-in-law dress me up in their trendy clothes and laugh at me telling people I'm 65. They think I should be proud to say I'm 80.

They approve of my young boyfriend, but I think that is only because they are not aware we are having sex. I feel they may be critical of this. The generation gap in reverse!

Chapter Ten

When Sex is Painful

Women who have experienced pain during intercourse and have tried to seek help often get a dreadful run-around. They are told by their doctor that the problem is probably psychological, and they are just as likely to be told by a psychologist that it is physical. There is probably some truth in both opinions, but this doesn't make it easy for the patient to determine what's wrong, and what to do about it.

Painful intercourse usually falls into two stages. The first stage is when the person first experiences pain. This is usually triggered by a physical problem. The second stage is the maintenance of the pain, and this can often be psychological.

PHYSICAL REASONS FOR PAINFUL INTERCOURSE

The location of the pain is a very good guide to the possible physical causes. In the table that follows on page 148, we provide an outline of some of the common reasons for pain in particular sites.

Physical Reasons for Painful Intercourse

WHEN	WHERE	WHY
Before intercourse during foreplay.	Outside on lips of vagina.	Skin diseases. Arthritis.
As penis enters vagina.	Entrance to vagina.	Infection irritation. Urinary tract infection. Postmenopausal changes to vagina. Scars from trauma or due to long-standing problems. Result of pregnancy.
Penis is mid-vagina.	Vagina and other internal structures.	Cystitis. Vaginitis. Scars. Postmenopausal changes. Disease in anus.
Deep penetration.	Cervix. Rectum. Lower back, hips. Lower abdomen.	Endometriosis. Cystitis. Postmenopause. Disease in anus. Orthopaedic problems. Result of pregnancy.
During orgasm.	Deep pelvis. Lower back. Lower abdomen.	Endometriosis. Scars in vagina. Scars from abdominal operations.
After intercourse.	Deep pelvis. Abdominal wall. Lower back.	Endometriosis. Abdominal scars (hernia). Vaginal scars.

This table may not list all possible physical problems that result in pain during intercourse, but it does suggest that a general practitioner should do exhaustive examinations before assuming that the person presenting with the problem is imagining it.

If you have been to your doctor with painful intercourse and haven't been given a thorough physical examination, you should return and ask for one. As you can see from the table, the pain could be in bone tissue (arthritis) or in muscle or ligaments, particularly in the pelvic area, and it could be due to: infections on the skin or within the vagina; past operations in any area of the pelvis; endometriosis or a result of pregnancy; lesions, adherences or scars on the vagina walls; urinary tract or anorectal diseases or problems; or a number of other less common complications.

Many sex therapists see clients who have been referred by their doctor because of painful intercourse, but have not had a proper physical examination. It is obviously pointless treating someone psychologically if the cause is physical. However, if the physical cause is not treated, the sufferer may also develop psychological problems.

PSYCHOLOGICAL REASONS FOR PAINFUL INTERCOURSE

The first and most simple psychological reason for painful intercourse can be lack of experience. This can lead to several lovemaking difficulties, such as: the male partner just pushing his penis into the vagina instead of

◁Reproduced from *Handbook of Sex Therapy*, by A. R. Arbanel, L. Lo Piccolo and J. Lo Piccolo, Plenum Press, 1978.

guiding it with his hand; pubic hair getting caught or pulled at the beginning of intercourse; lack of lubrication for the woman, because she isn't sufficiently aroused; the penis thrusting in a position that hits the woman's cervix; or the clitoris being rubbed too vigorously.

These problems can be simply dealt with by changing the approach to lovemaking and by broadening the couple's information about sex. This can include simple suggestions, such as: the male or female should guide the erect penis into the vagina; cut pubic hair or ensure it doesn't get caught; learn about ways in which the woman can be aroused before intercourse begins; the woman should tell her partner if any clitoral stimulation is unpleasant; and the couple should try different positions in intercourse — such as the woman on top — so that the thrusting of the penis doesn't cause pain.

If you have, however, been through that distressing cycle of feeling pain during intercourse then in vain attempting to find an answer — trooping round to doctors and being told that it might be psychological and to relax during sex, or, worse, being given tranquillisers — then you have probably, over time, got yourself into a pain trap. This means that because you have been so tense and worried about why you have had this problem you have developed psychological feelings of pain. Perhaps you have begun to doubt your relationship, or yourself, or begun to feel that no one can help, and that things will go on like this forever. All these concerns lead you to feel tense and unhappy. And you will probably also worry about experiencing the pain again, next time you have sex. This becomes a self-fulfilling prophesy, and sex ends in disappointment once again.

First of all, you should be persistent and get a number of opinions from medical people until you are able to establish the physical problem. As you can see from the earlier discussion, extensive examination may be necessary. Many doctors will often assume that the pain is psychological and brush you off with a brief examination. You will need to be assertive or seek another opinion to get to the explanation of the pain.

You may have discovered the physical problem and have since been given a clean bill of health, but found that the pain remains. This is probably psychological pain. But this doesn't mean your pain isn't real, or that you are going crazy. Pain is a very interesting phenomenon. There is no way we can measure it, and everyone experiences pain differently, at different times. Sometimes people can be seriously wounded and not experience any pain; in fact, they may be able to keep going as though nothing has happened. On the other hand, if someone has an injection, after waiting for some time, they may feel a disproportionate amount of pain. In other words, if you focus all your attention on the pain and begin to tense in anticipation you will notice it far more than if you are accidentally injured during some activity.

If you say to someone, 'I am going to prick you with this pin and it will hurt', and then you just touch them with your finger, they will probably flinch. Your finger might have felt like a pin-prick because the other person was anticipating pain.

How does all this relate to our discussion? Well, if you have, over a number of weeks, months or even years, continued to have a sexual relationship despite a physical problem that caused pain you will have learnt to associate pain with intercourse or sex. Even when the cause of the pain is under control your anticipation may lead you to continue to experience it. Getting annoyed with yourself will only increase your tension and make the pain worse. Instead, you need to break the cycle of associating sex with pain.

Ideally, this cycle would be easier to break if you didn't continue to have sex while you were in pain and if your partner were able to be supportive, if somewhat bewildered and frustrated. Then it would be a simple matter of learning to prevent yourself from getting tense, and to distract yourself at the stage when you used to experience pain.

To prevent yourself becoming tense, practise saying to yourself something like this:

'I know I have experienced pain in the past, and this means I will feel uncomfortable now, but focusing on and worrying about the pain will only make it worse. I will concentrate on my enjoyment and arousal.'

You will need to say this to yourself every time you think about pain or become tense during sex.

You and your partner will need to focus on enjoyable aspects of sex, making sure that you are both aroused and desire intercourse before proceeding. If you feel tense, stop what you are doing and do something else. Don't persist or you will probably feel pain again. It is helpful if your partner has the attitude of, 'I will help and be understanding, but I am not going to allow either of us to avoid this problem'. In other words, your partner should try to walk the delicate balance between pushing you to go a bit further, and yet not pushing too much. Remember, you can arouse each other and give each other an orgasm in many ways. You don't need intercourse to enjoy yourselves sexually.

Time and patience will enable you to eventually be comfortable in intercourse again. Being prepared to take things slowly and enjoy yourselves at the same time will be rewarded in the long run. One day you will have intercourse, enjoy it, and not even think about pain. You will reach this stage if you are prepared to persist with the simple guidelines given here.

Painful intercourse can have a string of unfortunate repercussions. If you were lucky enough, early on, to see a doctor who took your complaint seriously, who gave you a thorough examination and then outlined successful treatment including advice and information on how to cope with pain, then your prognosis is very good. Even if you had to seek a number of medical opinions before you were able to gain the appropriate medical, and then psychological, advice that enabled you both to work on the problem reasonably quickly, then your prognosis is good. Unfortunately, though, you may be one of the many people who hasn't been able to get a satisfactory answer for the pain, who is disillusioned with all medical advice and who feels brushed off by doctors and ignored. By the time people in this situation get into therapy with a psychologist they may have spent years with an unsatisfactory sex life. They have probably started to argue or become very tense and upset about sex, with bad effects on the rest of their relationship. By the time they seek help, this relationship may also be at risk. If you are in this position you and your partner should definitely seek professional psychological help. It may take longer to work on your problems because the relationship also needs help, but it could be well worth the effort in the long run. Refer to the back of the book for Recommended Reading and Support Organisations.

Stress may also be your problem: either stress because you have sexual difficulties, or stress from outside your relationship. Going back to our example of waiting for the doctor to give you an injection: if you are at all tense for any reason, even if it is just because you were late, the injection will feel more painful than if you are relaxed and comfortable. Similarly, if you are tense from rushing around, you can't expect to suddenly jump into bed and relax and enjoy yourself. In other words, a stressful lifestyle may be a contributing factor to your sexual problem.

Stress can also result in the continuation of infections and diseases that have been the cause of your pain during intercourse. For instance, thrush can be a continual nuisance if the person is stressed, and herpes is more likely to recur under stress. The reason for this is that when you become stressed (which basically means you feel run-down and tired and you are trying to cope with too much) it affects your immune system, making it less efficient.

If you are under stress then you will need to seek advice from a psychologist, or begin by reading some appropriate self-help books (see Recommended Reading).

Question

I get pain that feels like a hot rod inside me during intercourse. This has gone on for a few years.

Recently I had an operation to have torn tissue removed from around the vagina, and the doctor made the opening a little larger, thinking this would also help me.

However, everything is still the same. I've been back to the doctor three times. Each time he says to give it more time to settle down. He has likened it to women after childbirth having painful intercourse for the first few weeks. But I know the pain is exactly the same as it was before the operation. He won't listen to me. He hasn't examined me physically since the operation, and I'm too depressed to remind him he should. Can you offer any advice?

Answer

Time to change doctors by the sound of things. You could have anything wrong with you from a low-grade infection to scar tissue. Or it could be lesions that open up during intercourse, then, after a few days, close over again — leaving no sign of anything in the vagina that would have caused the pain. These are just a couple of possibilities. You must get an understanding, patient doctor who is prepared to listen to everything you say and make sure there is no physical problem. And he must be able to convince you of this. It is possible after you have had painful intercourse that the expectation of pain the next time, will cause you to feel it (as discussed above).

Question

My girlfriend is only having sex to please me; she is in constant pain during intercourse. We've been together for twelve months, but in the last two months she has been in agony. Before that everything was fine. She has not been to a doctor yet.

Answer

A medical opinion is essential for both of you. There are a number of infections she could have, or you could have, which can be passed back and forth. Endometriosis is another possibility. Without a doctor seeing you both there is no real way of knowing why she has the pain. But it is certainly an indication that there is something wrong.

Question

As soon as I enter my girlfriend she becomes dry and scratchy. I also get rashes all over my penis after sex with her. It is very painful, so we use vaseline. She hasn't had a period for four years.

Answer

See a doctor immediately about a possible infection as well as her menstruation. Don't use petroleum-based lubricants; rather, try KY Jelly or Lubifax. Ask your chemist for appropriate lubricants.

Question

When I have sex with my husband I get shooting pains in my abdomen, and there is hurt in my vagina. What is causing it?

I was a virgin when we married a year ago, and the pain started from the very first time we had intercourse. I have tried different positions, with no relief. There is not much lubrication, so I suppose arousal is not as high as it should be. I have never had an orgasm. A doctor has checked me, and all he could point to as a possible cause of the pain was that my uterus is tipped back slightly.

I think the problem might be somehow connected with my childhood, when I was handled sexually by a male friend of my parents. I remember it vividly. It went on for some time. Another reason could be my hopeless body image. My mother always tormented me about my sexuality. She would laugh about my body to other people, and in front of me. My marriage is under a deal of strain. We argue a lot.

Answer

You could be finding it hard to trust your husband during sex (and are therefore unable to lose control enough to reach orgasm), because your trust was shattered as a little girl when you were sexually abused. This can lead to lack of arousal and consequent painful intercourse. Obviously, your mother's criticism plays a major role if you see yourself as she describes you. The vicious cycle of arguments and painful sex will continue unless you meet the problem head on, that is, see a psychologist.

Once you take some action you will start to feel better, because you will be turning this awful tide. Make sure your husband is included in this counselling otherwise he will feel more and more alienated from you and the relationship. (See also Chapter 11.)

Question

My girlfriend won't have sex with me, and that's all right because I don't believe in sex before marriage. For the same reason I don't want to masturbate — I think it is wrong. However, we can't help kissing and touching a bit. After these sessions I get so painful in the groin that I can hardly walk. Should I see a doctor?

Answer

This is due to congestion in the testes from the engorged blood vessels. Researchers believe that more men suffer this in silence than the numbers willing to admit it. It is believed that men who maintain an erection for great lengths of time during intercourse also experience this pain. See a doctor, by all means, if you are still worried.

Question

I fell over and cut myself on the penis about four weeks ago. It was not very deep, but it bled a lot. The problem now is that when I get an erection, the scab comes off. Of course this slows down the healing process somewhat. What can I do?

Answer

Short of not getting an erection, unless your doctor can

prescribe something to speed up the healing process, there is not much you can do, unfortunately. Definitely worth another visit to the doctor though.

Listeners Share Experiences

I'm quite upset because I have hurt my girlfriend during intercourse. Possibly, she was a virgin. I just wish it had not happened. We still see each other, but everything is different. There is an air of discomfort between us. I want to know if she is better, but can't bring myself to ask her.

Since my hysterectomy about five years ago I have had a dry vagina, which naturally hurts when I have sex. My doctor has prescribed an icy gel which I can only use ten days at a time. That helps, but on the weeks I have to lay off using it the problem is still there. When I have the problem, I also have pain in the lower back. Everything was taken away during my hysterectomy.

This may sound silly, but I think my girlfriend's vagina is splitting. When we have sex she produces no lubrication at all. Lovemaking has all but ceased because it hurts her so much. However, when I want to talk about it — suggest a doctor, creams, etc. — she just gets angry and refuses to talk. I definitely feel left out, and somehow guilty about the pain. The whole thing has shot the rest of the relationship to pieces. I try not to think this is the finish, but I suspect she is using this to get out of the relationship. I don't want that to happen.

Chapter Eleven

Sexual Assault

This subject came up on the program only occasionally, usually in calls from distraught, angry, sad callers. However, it always brought great response from listeners.

Looking back, some of the most distressing calls came from people who were being, or had been, sexually assaulted. One call in particular, from a young girl, will remain with us for a very long time. This is what she said on air.

My parents are overseas and they have left me with my uncle. He is forcing me to have sex with him. I'm 16.

He has never done this before; he's always been really good. He says that if I tell anyone, he'll say I wanted to do it, and he'll ring my mother and tell her I am doing it willingly. He blames it on me because he says that I keep turning him on.

I am too scared to move. Anyway I don't want to tell my girlfriend. I'm alone because all our family is in England. He said if I do go to stay with my friend he will make all his mates do it with me.

I don't want to tell anyone, no one would believe me . . .

At this point, Rebecca, as she called herself on air, with urgency bordering on hysteria, kept repeating, 'I have to go, I have to go'. And from the background, clearly, we could hear the angry voice of a man say, 'Put that bloody phone down!'. Then the line went dead.

What happened to Rebecca that night we, and those listening, could only imagine. It made us all witnesses to the chilling horror of child sexual abuse.

Despite appeals on radio and television programs in the next couple of weeks, we never found her and therefore were unable to help her.

Other calls came from teenage boys who felt unhappy and manipulated because they had gone along with sexual advances from teachers and were now being emotionally blackmailed, and from women who had been abused in their early years and had had difficulty handling relationships in their adult life. There were also calls from mothers who were concerned about the effects of sexual abuse on their children.

As a society we have only recently begun to recognise the extent of sexual abuse that occurs in our community. We have also just begun to recognise and acknowledge that the abuse is rarely from strangers, but more often from someone the child or adult knows. In the past, of course, children were warned about the dangers of talking to or being persuaded into a car by a stranger, but they were not told that a relative or friend could be the perpetrator of a sexual offence. This wall of silence about the more likely offenders must have increased the trauma for assault victims. They must have felt as though they were the only ones attracting the attentions of a friend or relative, and this would have increased their feelings of isolation and guilt.

In a more enlightened age, we can only hope that more and more victims can be helped to recognise that what is being done to them is wrong, and that the only way to end the situation is to speak up about it. There are many complex issues involved in sexual assault, which is perhaps why this problem has been shrouded in silence for so long. We shall now take a look at those issues, the effects of sexual assault, what to do about it, and how to prevent it.

IIOW DO I HELP MY CHILDREN AVOID SEXUAL ASSAULT?

No one can protect their children 24 hours a day, particularly if the abusing adult is a trusted friend or member of the family. But there are three main ways you can help your children to help themselves if approached sexually by an adult.

BE APPROACHABLE
Probably the most important factor in preventing or short-circuiting sexual abuse of your children is *your* relationship with them. Try to foster a good open relationship with them, and to be approachable, no matter what the problem is. All parents get angry sometimes — often justifiably — but try and show that, despite this, you always try to be fair and understanding, and willing to listen to your children's viewpoint. Even if you don't feel calm, try and deal with whatever comes up in a reasonable way.

If you can manage this, you have laid a foundation of trust that will enable your children to come to you, no matter how much trouble they are in. Conversely, if you always 'go off the deep end' when they are in trouble, they are far less likely to ask for your help in serious situations.

In other words, your child needs to know you are not just a 'fair weather' parent, who is helpful when things go well, but who overreacts or becomes unreasonable when things go wrong. There must be a sense of solidity in your relationship before your children feel they can rely on you in a crisis. If you feel you need some help in developing this kind of relationship, see the books listed under Recommended Reading.

One of the major components of the sexual abuse of children is the emotional blackmail applied by the abuser, and the consequent feeling of intimacy because of a shared secret, on the part of the child. A child who doesn't feel he or she has solid emotional support from someone outside the abusing situation will be far more vulnerable to both the blackmail and the intimacy than a child who feels he or she can confide in a parent.

TALK FRANKLY ABOUT SEX

From a very early age, at a level appropriate to your child's understanding, you should talk frankly about questions related to sex. A child who has some knowledge of the basic facts about sex is, again, far less vulnerable than the one who knows nothing about sexual behaviour.

Many children who have been sexually abused are confused and uncertain about what the adult has asked them to do. Through lack of sexual education they don't recognise sexual behaviour. On the one hand, they may quite enjoy the sexual stimulation but, on the other hand, they don't quite know what it's all about, and sense that it's shameful in some way.

DISCUSS SEXUAL ABUSE

As part of your general discussion of sex, talk about sexual abuse, and discuss what your child should do if an adult makes a sexual advance.

There are a number of anti-child-abuse programs

around that discuss how to teach your children about this. The basis of most programs is that you should encourage your children to see themselves as having control over their own bodies, and to feel they have the right to tell adults that they don't want to be held or touched in certain ways, or at certain times.

Discuss with your children the difference between 'okay' touching and touching that is not all right — giving guidelines of acceptable and unacceptable touching.

Having encouraged your children to say no if they don't like being touched in a certain way, you, as parents, must also accept your child's right to reject your affectionate advances if he or she does not feel like being hugged or kissed by you. The same applies to family friends and grandparents: you should not urge your children to hug or kiss another person if they don't feel like it. Obviously, this could be the cause of some embarrassment — particularly with grandparents — but in the long run your children will be better off because they will have learnt to be assertive about the giving and receiving of affection. This will not only help to prevent or short-circuit unwanted sexual advances, but will also help them develop healthy sexual relationships in the future.

Finally, you can plan with your children what they would do if someone — whether it is someone they know or a stranger — persists in touching them after they have indicated they don't want to be touched. An American anti-child-abuse program recommends the simple procedure of teaching your child to yell 'No!', call another adult immediately and then tell you, the parent, what has happened.

BEHAVIOUR TO WATCH

Children who are being sexually abused will often suddenly start to behave in unacceptable ways. Friendly and outgoing children may become withdrawn and unresponsive, or loud and aggressive. Children who did well at school may start to perform poorly.

Any child whose behaviour changes dramatically is probably disturbed about something. Of course, the problem is not necessarily sexual assault, but parents or some other caring adult should try to find out the reason for the change.

As we have already said, ideally, a child should be able to turn to a parent when he or she is in trouble. However, if you haven't been able to establish good communication with your child, but you see something is wrong, try and find someone he or she *is* willing to talk to.

Don't allow your child to put off disclosing what the upset is about but, at the same time, don't push him or her to tell you what the problem is straight away.

WHAT EFFECT DOES SEXUAL ASSAULT HAVE ON A CHILD?

The long-term effects are largely determined by whether or not the child is able to seek help from a trustworthy adult, and the degree of closeness of the relationship between the abusing adult and the child.

In cases where you, the parent, are able to short-circuit an adult's sexual advances on your child, minimal harm occurs. Similarly, even if the child is involved in sexual interaction with an adult, but is able to tell his or her parent straight away — and so put an end to the abuse — very little harm occurs.

However, it is far more harmful when the abused child feels he or she has no one to turn to, and has to somehow deal with this traumatic situation alone. Understandably, the child does not have the resources to do this. The situation is made worse by the abusing adult making threats about what will happen if the child tells anyone.

If the sexual abuse continues unchecked, and the child never seeks help from a caring adult, it can have devastating long-term effects on the child. As an adult he or she will almost certainly find it difficult to trust others and to make friends, and poor self-esteem will prevent the full development of his or her potential. Sexual difficulties may also occur in later life.

The closer the relationship between the child and his or her abuser, the more serious the harm will be. In cases where a parent, grandparent or some other important figure in the child's life is the abuser, it can cause untold damage to the child — particularly if no one intervenes.

A caring parent can be in a most difficult position if a spouse or close relative is abusing a child. But, for the sake of the child, the abuse must be brought out into the open and stopped.

What causes the damage to the child is not so much the sexual side of the abuse, but the abuse of the child's trust: the blackmailing of the child, playing on the child's fear ('Daddy might go to gaol, etc.').

It is questionable, particularly if the abuse goes on for any length of time, whether a child will ever fully recover. He or she can be helped to learn to cope, but will never be the same. It is much better to prevent than to ever let things reach this stage.

THE EFFECTS OF SEXUAL ASSAULT ON AN ADULT

An adult has more resources to cope with a sexual assault, but the effects can still be dramatic and may have long-standing repercussions. A sexually abused adult usually experiences the same feelings of guilt ('What did I do to deserve this?') and loss of trust ('Who can I trust now?'). Both these reactions have implications for how the person copes. The guilt tends to make the victim blame himself or herself for the attack. The person may begin to wonder what is wrong with himself or herself, and to withdraw or shy away from previous relationships. If friends and family are not able to understand this reaction, the situation becomes worse. The victim's lack of trust may also make him or her suspicious and nervous, which once again may not be understood by friends and family.

These reactions can sometimes last for over twelve months or more. Even when friends are supportive and understanding at first, their patience can wear very thin if the person doesn't seem to recover within a few months. If help isn't sought, these reactions may continue for years, creating many problems for the person who was assaulted.

A traumatic event like a sexual assault can also exacerbate pre-existing problems. If, for example, the person tended to have difficulty in social situations, this could become worse after an attack. Similarly, if the person had problems at work, these may be aggravated. So often the victim is left to deal not only with the effects of an attack, but also the worsening of a pre-existing problem. Professional help is often necessary for this reason.

HOW TO COPE WITH SEXUAL ASSAULT

If the victim is a child then his or her environment needs to be stabilised as soon as possible. There has been recent controversy about taking the child out of the home if abuse has been occurring within the family. This is probably as destructive as the abuse itself. The child needs to be given the opportunity to feel safe and to begin re-establishing trust in adults around him or her. This will not occur if the child is dragged out of the home and expected to live with strangers. Ideally, supervision and support should be given so that the family can stay together. If it is decided that the offending parent should go, it should be made very clear to the child that this isn't because of his or her revelation, but because of a decision made by the adults.

If the offender is a friend of the family or relative it will be necessary to speak to that person, and to give the child support and encouragement to speak up and tell if that person ever makes another sexual approach. The child should be encouraged to feel he or she can speak freely about his or her feelings.

If the child feels safe and happy, this will be demonstrated in his or her behaviour. There is no need to continue to discuss the issue if the child seems to have forgotten it, and is happy. You may, however, like to prepare yourself for talking about what happened, later in the child's life. In general, young children will express their feelings in their behaviour and you will be able to judge if they are still upset by what they do, rather than what they say. Once, as we have said, their environment is stabilised and they have been given some strategies for coping, their behaviour should begin returning to normal. If this doesn't happen seek professional guidance (see Support Organisations).

Most adults need plenty of time to express how badly they feel. It is difficult to put a time limit on such things but, generally speaking, you might expect a person to feel bad for three months, to start putting his or her life together over the next six months, and to have returned to normal after another three months. Over the first nine months his or her feelings may go up and down: one minute the person is happy and coping, the next depressed. As long as the person expects this and understands what is happening, he or she will survive this period. But if the person, or anyone around, begins to worry about this reaction, the situation usually becomes worse.

WHERE TO GO FOR HELP

Even if you decide not to press legal charges you should not hide the sexual assault from other people. It is necessary to get support and help during such a traumatic time. If you feel friends and relatives can't offer you the advice you feel you need, go and see a professional. If you are the parent of a child who has been abused, you may need more support and help than your child. NEVER be put off by people who say, 'You should be over this now. Pull yourself together'. Seek professional help.

There are now a number of sexual assault clinics, some of which are listed under Support Organisations. They are usually attached to major hospitals, and are also listed in the Yellow Pages. The people in these clinics are specifically trained to help with the effects of sexual assault. They will offer the support and help that friends may not be able to give. If you feel you have developed other personal problems since a sexual assault you may also have to see a clinical psychologist, either at the clinic or in private practice.

Probably everyone who has been involved in a sexual assault, or who is very close to someone who has been attacked, should seek professional help at least once — no matter how well they *seem* to be coping.

Question

My football coach and sports teacher asked me to stay back after practice at school to view a video. I thought it would be a video of the team, because I'm captain but it was of my teacher and another male teacher involved in unspeakable acts. I just walked out. But the next week after training, he tried to force himself on me sexually in the showers and, again, I just walked out. I couldn't find words to say anything because it was embarrassing and unexpected. Then he started saying he'd drop me from the team and really pressuring me until I gave in. Now I want to get out of it, and I can't. It has gone on for five weeks. I can see where I went wrong by giving in, and I want to get out of it. I'm 16. Can you help me?

Answer

We advised this boy that he first go to his parents, another adult, or the school counsellor to get him out of the immediate situation. We also suggested that he should follow that up with help from a sexual assault clinic.

The boy felt he could go to his school counsellor most comfortably. The important thing was to assure him that his reactions were quite normal, otherwise he could have experienced overwhelming guilt about giving in. The pressure he was put under, as well as the teacher's superior position, were what had made him give in. We did not hear what happened to this young student.

Question

I've been involved in a teacher–student sexual relationship. It started when the teacher passed me notes to meet her after school. As she is about twelve years older than me, I wasn't sure what was going on. Eventually it was clear that she was after me sexually. It put me in a real dilemma, but I gave in. I have to admit I was fascinated that she was interested in me, at first. Then I started to realise she was using me. She had an advantage over me at school because she could hold the relationship against me. It was awful.

I realised the best thing to do was get out of the situation at any cost. She threatened me with altering exam results, as it was just prior to exam time. She actually said I'd fail if I didn't continue with the sexual relationship. Finally, I have ended it by just refusing to see her any more. My big worry is what is going to happen next year, particularly with my exam results. She is directly responsible for my marks. I don't know where to turn right now. I've thought about telling my parents, but I don't know what they would say. What should I do?

Answer

The advice given here was for the caller to try really hard to tell his parents, recognising that their initial reaction would be one of shock. He needed some sort of back-up if the exam results were falsified and, as his relationship with his parents seemed good, it was possible they would be able to sort out the sexual blackmailing on the part of the teacher.

We pointed out that the notes she had passed him, which he had kept, would help support his case.

He turned out to be a very brave young man. The day after speaking to us on radio, he approached his parents by 'just blurting it out'. As we predicted, they were shocked. However, once over that, they took control and, when we last had contact from him, they had arranged a meeting with his headmaster.

Listeners Share Experiences

At a family gathering eighteen years ago an adult cousin took me into one of the bedrooms and, without saying anything, had sex with me. I didn't even understand what he was doing, I was only eight. Despite this, I felt then — and still do — that I was dirty.

He spoke when it was over. All he said was, 'It's okay, it's all right'. I am having psychological help. While it hasn't really screwed me up, it is always there. I can't go to bed with a man without first having a drink and few little things like that.

I was shattered to learn that my sister had been abused by the same man who had endlessly abused me. I was coping quite well with the memory of my own terrible time until she broke down and told me what had happened.

We are adults now, in our thirties. I love her very much, and the thought that she had endured those terrible, terrible things, too, is just too much for me to bear.

The man was an uncle who moved in to help out my mother when our father died. We are a southern

171

European family and were recent migrants to this country at the time. His son also abused me.

I kept it to myself because I felt so bad and also because my parents had had such a hard life in Europe, and then my mother having to cope with my father's death.

Everyone thought what a wonderful man this uncle was to take care of his brother's family the way he did. My mother was singing his praises a few weeks ago and, after all this time of keeping quiet, I screamed at her what he had done. She was very shocked — particularly that we had not been to her about it. I think I need help now.

Instead of going to school one day, my 15-year-old son went to the beach. At the end of his day of wagging it, when he was getting out of his bathers and back into his school clothes, he was sexually abused by an adult man who had been in the changing rooms.

My son came home to an empty house, because I was shopping. When I got in he was hysterical. He eventually told me what happened. I comforted him and went to ring the police. While I was doing this he went into the bathroom and took an overdose of drugs prescribed for another member of the family.

This may appear melodramatic, or difficult to believe, but it is exactly how it happened. I am telling it in support of other ordinary, happy Australian families who have had this horror thrust upon them.

On top of the trauma my son had already suffered that day, he also had to deal with the police, an ambulance ride and doctors.

I can honestly say that he has been affected by that dreadful experience to this very day. He is 25, and relationships with women are out of the question. He has seen psychologists and he is able to talk with me about it. My husband and I will never give up supporting him and trying to help him. My fear is that he will one day decide it is not worth the struggle any more.

No matter what I do, I can't shift the horror of having been abused by my father from my mind. I have deliberately blocked out anything that happened before I was 15.

There was physical abuse as well as sexual, consequently I have never laid a hand on my own children. He even threatened to kill me.

No amount of psychological help has been able to dislodge the feelings of unworthiness, fear, guilt and anger.

I have been in trouble with the law but, fortunately, got off. It was an impulsive act on my part. I feel that I don't know what I want most of the time.

I was raped by a female friend of my mother when I was ten. She often babysat, and this is when it would happen. I felt totally dominated by her, although at that age I wasn't sure what was going on. My mum is a single mother and I feel a bit reluctant to raise the subject.

This woman still visits, and she threatens to say I was the one involving her — not the other way around — if I tell. It hasn't happened for the last twelve months. I'm 15 now.

When I was about 14, I was forced into sex for a period of time, with a member of the clergy. He coerced me into it by making me feel guilty, telling me I really wanted to participate, and accusing me of encouraging him by how I looked. I was 14, for heaven's sake, and not a very sophisticated child — I hardly looked in the mirror, let alone had the awareness to be encouraging a man old enough to be my grandfather. Now that I am in my sixties, I realise

173

there were people around me then who would have helped, had I not been so trapped in my terror. But it has taken almost this long to realise that.

I'm proof that you can come through sexual molestation. When I was 11 my father started to have sex with me. There were a lot of family problems associated with it. Eventually I met my husband and, from that time, things started to go right. He knew what had happened before we got married. We tried to work our problems out ourselves, but it got too hard to do. So I finally sought counselling and am now in a support group. And it's just terrific.

On reflection, making the decision to get counselling was the hardest part. I knew there were a lot of problems to go back to and sort out, but once I had made the commitment I was all right.

The support group has been the real breakthrough. The most important discovery for me was knowing I was not alone in thinking, 'I'm this terrible person, and no one else has ever gone through this'. We had all experienced that. We help each other through all the problems, fear, hurt, guilt, and mistrust. Also the lack of confidence. Even though outwardly I appeared to be a supremely confident, calm person, deep down I was a trembling mess.

I avoid my father where possible. My mother will ring and put me on the phone to him and I have to say hello, but that is all. My mother only found out a couple of years ago, and her attitude is, 'Forget it and get on with your life, because it happened so long ago'. But you can't, unless you deal with it.

The fact that my mother rejects my account of what happened and wants to brush it away has made me very angry, but I've come to the conclusion it is her problem now. I have protected her long enough. I'll come through, I know I will.

Support Organisations

FAMILY PLANNING ASSOCIATIONS

AUSTRALIAN CAPITAL TERRITORY
Health Promotion Centre
Childers St
Canberra 2601
Tel: (062) 47 3077

NEW SOUTH WALES
161 Broadway
Sydney 2007
Tel: (02) 211 0244
    (02) 698 9499

NORTHERN TERRITORY
133 Mitchell St
Larrakeyah 5790
Tel: (089) 81 5335

QUEENSLAND
100 Alfred St
Fortitude Valley 4006
Tel: (07) 252 5151

SOUTH AUSTRALIA
17 Phillips St
Kensington 5068
Tel (08) 31 5177

TASMANIA
73 Federal St
North Hobart 7002
Tel: (002) 34 7200

VICTORIA
266–270 Church St
Richmond 3121
Tel: (03) 429 1177

Action Centre
Adolescent Counselling
268 Flinders Lane
Melbourne 3000
Tel: (03) 654 4766

WESTERN AUSTRALIA
104 Collins St
West Perth 6005
Tel: (09) 321 2701

SEXUALLY TRANSMITTED DISEASES CLINICS

AUSTRALIAN CAPITAL TERRITORY
Woden Valley Hospital
Canberra 2601
Tel: (062) 84 2184

NEW SOUTH WALES
Nightingale Centre
Sydney Hospital
Macquarie St
Sydney 2000
Tel: (02) 27 3634
 (02) 27 4851

NORTHERN TERRITORY
Royal Darwin Hospital
Darwin 5790
Tel: (089) 20 7211

QUEENSLAND
484 Adelaide St
Brisbane 4000
Tel: (07) 227 7091
 (07) 227 7095

SOUTH AUSTRALIA
275 North Tce
Adelaide 5000
Tel: (08) 226 6025

TASMANIA
Royal Hobart Hospital
Hobart 7000
Tel: (002) 38 8308

VICTORIA
364 Little Lonsdale St
Melbourne 3000
Tel: (03) 602 4900
 (03) 602 4540

WESTERN AUSTRALIA
74 Murray St
Perth 6000
Tel: (09) 220 1122

AIDS CLINICS AND COUNSELLING CENTRES

AUSTRALIAN CAPITAL TERRITORY
STD Clinic
Woden Valley Hospital
Canberra 2601
Tel: (062) 84 2184

AIDS Council
8 Lonsdale St
Braddon 2601
Tel: (062) 57 2855

NEW SOUTH WALES
Albion Street Clinic
150–154 Albion St
Surry Hills 2010
Tel: (02) 332 4000
 (008) 02 3300

AIDS Council
68 Sophia St
Surry Hills 2010
Tel: (02) 211 0499
 (02) 212 2728

NORTHERN TERRITORY
STD Clinic
Royal Darwin Hospital
Darwin 5790
Tel: (089) 20 7211

AIDS Council
1st Floor
Burns Philp Building
cnr Huckey and Smith sts
Darwin 0800
Tel: (089) 41 1711

QUEENSLAND
STD Clinic
484 Adelaide St
Brisbane 4000
Tel: (07) 227 7091
    (Male)
    (07) 227 7095
    (Female)

AIDS Council
546 Stanley St
Mater Hill 4101
Tel: (07) 844 1990

SOUTH AUSTRALIA
STD Clinic
275 North Tce
Adelaide 5000
Tel: (08) 226 6025

AIDS Council
3/130 Carrington St
Adelaide 5000
Tel: (08) 223 6322

TASMANIA
STD Clinic
Royal Hobart Hospital
Hobart 7000
Tel: (002) 38 8308

AIDS Council
2/343B Elizabeth St
Hobart 7000
Tel: (002) 31 1930

VICTORIA
STD Clinic
364 Little Lonsdale St
Melbourne 3000
Tel: (03) 602 4900
    (03) 602 3002

AIDS Council
117 Johnston St
Collingwood 3066
Tel: (03) 417 1759

WESTERN AUSTRALIA
Special Treatment Clinic
74 Murray St
Perth 6000
Tel: (09) 220 1122

AIDS Council
Suite 5
85 Stirling St
Northbridge 6000
Tel: (09) 227 8355

SEXUAL ASSAULT HELP CENTRES

AUSTRALIAN CAPITAL TERRITORY
Domestic Violence Crisis
Service
PO Box 320
Civic Square
Canberra 2608
Tel: (062) 47 8022
(062) 48 7800
(Crisis Line)

NEW SOUTH WALES
Royal Prince Alfred Sexual
Assault Centre
King George V Hospital
Missenden Rd
Camperdown 2050
Tel: (02) 516 8131
(02) 516 6111 (AH)

Child Abuse Team
The Children's Hospital
Camperdown 2050
Tel: (02) 692 6624
(02) 519 0466 (AH)

Sexual Assault Centre
Royal North Shore Hospital
Pacific Highway
St Leonards 2065
Tel: (02) 438 7580
(02) 438 7111 (AH)

Child Abuse Team
Prince of Wales Hospital
High St
Randwick 2031
Tel: (02) 399 4413

Sexual Assault Centre
St George Hospital
Belgrave St
Kogarah 2217
Tel: (02) 588 1111

Westmead Sexual Assault
Centre
Grevillea Cottage
Westmead Hospital
Westmead 2145
Tel: (02) 633 7940
(02) 633 6333 (AH)

Whitlam Sexual Assault
Service
Community Health Centre
205 Northumberland St
Liverpool 2170
Tel: (02) 601 2333

NORTHERN TERRITORY
Ms Kathy Munroe
Counsellor/Social Worker
Sexual Assault Centre
Royal Darwin Hospital
PO Box 41326
Casuarina 5792
Tel: (089) 20 7211

QUEENSLAND
The Collective
Rape Crisis Centre
The Women's House
30 Victoria St
West End 4010
Tel: (07) 844 4008

SOUTH AUSTRALIA
Co-ordinator
Sexual Assault Referral Centre
Queen Elizabeth Hospital
Woodville Rd
Woodville 5110
Tel: (08) 45 0222

TASMANIA
Sexual Assault Support
Service Inc.
PO Box 217
North Hobart 7000
Tel: (002) 31 1811

VICTORIA
Sexual Assault Clinic
Monash Medical Centre
PO Locked Bag 29
Clayton 3168
Tel: (03) 550 2289

Centre Against Sexual Assault
CASA House
270 Cardigan St
Carlton 3053
Tel: (03) 344 2210

North-east Sexual Assault
Centre
Austin Hospital
Upper Heidelberg Rd
Heidelberg 3084
Tel: (03) 450 5770

Western Region Centre Against
Sexual Assault
17 Eleanor St
Footscray 3011
Tel: (03) 318 5222

Royal Children's Hospital
Child Protection Team
Social Work Department
Flemington Rd
Parkville 3052
Tel: (03) 345 5522

WESTERN AUSTRALIA
Sexual Assault Referral Centre
411 Barker Rd
Subiaco 6008
Tel: (09) 382 3323
     (09) 381 6333

Child Sexual Assault Clinic
Princess Margaret Hospital
Thomas St
Subiaco 6008
Tel: (09) 38 2822

SEXUAL GUIDANCE CLINICS

Most major public hospitals have a sexual guidance clinic. Call the main number and ask for the clinic.

MENOPAUSE CLINICS

Some women's hospitals have a menopause clinic. Call the main number and ask for the clinic.

PSYCHOLOGISTS

The Australian Psychological Society will provide names of clinical psychologists in your area. Call the branch of the Society in your capital city and ask for the name of a psychologist with clinical experience in sexual therapy.

PLASTIC SURGEONS

The Australian Society of Plastic Surgeons will provide names of relevant fully trained plastic surgeons in your area. Call the number of the branch of the Society in your capital city.

Recommended Reading

SEXUALLY TRANSMITTED DISEASES

Bradford, David. *A.I.D.S., Herpes and Everything You Should Know About V.D. in Australia*. Melbourne University Press, 1985.

CONTRACEPTION

Australian Federation of Family Planning Associations. *Choices in Family Planning*. Australian Federation of Family Planning Associations, 1985.

Billings, Evelyn & Westmore, Ann. *The Billings Method: Controlling Fertility without Drugs or Devices*. Anne O'Donovan, 1988.

Pfeiffer, R. & Whitlock, K. *Fertility Awareness: How to Become Pregnant When You Want to and Avoid Pregnancy When You Don't*. Prentice-Hall, 1984.

ADOLESCENT SEXUALITY

Claesson, Bert. *Boy–Girl–Man–Woman*. M. Boyers, 1982.

Mayle, Peter & Robbins, Arthur. *We're Not Pregnant: An Illustrated Guide to Birth Control*. Sun Books, 1981.

Wellings, Kay. *First Love, First Sex: Practical Guide to Relationships*. Greenhouse, 1986.

Wootten, Vicki. *Be Yourself: Love, Sex and You*. Penguin, 1989.

SEX EDUCATION

Hite, S. *The Hite Report: A Nationwide Study of Female Sexuality.* Cassell, 1979.

Hite, S. *The Hite Report on Male Sexuality.* Ballantine, 1981.

Katchadourian, H. *Human Sexuality: Sense and Nonsense.* Norton, 1979.

Llewellyn-Jones, Derek. *Everywoman.* Faber and Faber, 1986.

Llewellyn-Jones, Derek. *Everyman.* Oxford University Press, 1987.

Mayle, P. *Where Did I Come From?* Sun Books, 1975.

Mayle, P. *What's Happening to Me?* Sun Books, 1980.

Zilbergeld, B. *Male Sexuality: A Guide to Sexual Fulfillment.* Bantam Books, 1984.

The following cassette is available from ABRA, 3 Alexandra Parade, Collingwood, Victoria 3066: Montgomery, Bob & Cooper, Muriel. *Sex Education*.

SEXUAL PROBLEMS

Arbanel, A.R., Lo Piccolo, L. & Lo Piccolo, J. *Handbook of Sex Therapy.* Plenum Press, 1978.

Arndt, Bettina. *Female Sexual Expression.* Applied Behavioural Research Association, 1976.

Gochros, H. & Fisher, J. *Treat Yourself to a Better Sex Life.* Prentice-Hall, 1980.

Heiman, Julia & Lo Piccolo, Joseph. *Becoming Orgasmic: A Sexual Growth Program for Women.* Prentice-Hall, 1988.

OTHER PROBLEMS

Jakubowski, P. & Lange, A. *The Assertive Option: Your Rights and Responsibilities*. Research Press, 1978.

Lever, J. *P.M.T.: The Unrecognized Illness*. Outback Press, 1979.

Montgomery, Bob & Evans, Lynette. *You and Stress*. Viking O'Neil, 1989.

Phelps, Stanlee & Austin, Nancy. *The Assertive Woman*. Impact, 1987.

Phillips, G. *Help for Shy People*. Prentice-Hall, 1981.

IMPROVING RELATIONSHIPS

Comfort, Alex. *The Joy of Sex*. Crown Publications, 1972.

Fisher, B. *Rebuilding: When Your Relationship Ends*. Impact Publications, 1981.

Gochros, H. & Fisher, J. *Treat Yourself to a Better Sex Life*. Prentice-Hall, 1980.

Gottman, John et al. *A Couple's Guide to Communication*. Research Press, 1986.

Montgomery, Bob & Evans, Lynette. *Living and Loving Together*. Viking O'Neil, 1989.

Montgomery, Bob & Morris, Laurel. *You and Sex*. Nelson, 1987.

SEXUAL ASSAULT

Adams, C. & Fay, J. *No More Secrets: Protecting Your Child from Sexual Assault*. Impact, 1981.

Adams, C., Fay, J. & Loreen-Martin, J. *No is Not Enough: Helping Teenagers Avoid Sexual Assault*. Impact, 1984.

Huchton, Laura M. *Protect Your Child: A Parent's Safeguard Against Child Abduction and Sexual Abuse*. Prentice-Hall, 1985.